Zoo Animals
A Smithsonian Guide

Key to Zoo Animals

Monkeys   p. 32   Chimpanzees p. 44   Gorillas   p. 56   Parrots   p. 59

Tropical Forests

Elephants   p. 70   Rhinos   p. 72   Giraffes   p. 76   Zebras   p. 77

Grasslands

Cheetah   p. 80   Lion   p. 81   Foxes   p. 104   Snakes   p. 118

Deserts

Deciduous Forests

Coniferous Forests   **Mountains**

Permanent Ice and Tundra

Zoo Animals
A Smithsonian Guide

Michael H. Robinson
Director of the National Zoo

David Challinor
Science Advisor to the Secretary
Smithsonian Institution

with
Holly Webber

Macmillan • USA

Macmillan • USA

A Simon & Schuster Macmillan Company
15 Columbus Circle
New York, NY 10023

A Latimer Book

In the Gallery

page 1.   Ling-Ling, a giant panda at the National Zoo, chews on leafy bamboo stalks.
pages 2–3. The Bengal tiger's dark stripes enable it to hide easily in the tropical forest.
pages 4–5. With her baby clinging to her back, a female orangutan feeds on leaves.
pages 6–7. The rocky Alaska coastline provides resting spots for puffins.
page 10.   A young giraffe peers out from underneath its mother's belly.
page 11.   A shaggy-maned male lion rests quietly beneath a tree.
page 13.   Pink-plumed flamingos are a colorful sight at the Miami MetroZoo.

Library of Congress Cataloging-in-Publication Data

Robinson, Michael H.
  Zoo Animals: A Smithsonian Guide / Michael H. Robinson, David Challinor
    p.   cm.   (Smithsonian Guides)
    "A Latimer book."
    Includes bibliographical references and index.
    ISBN 0-02-860406-7 ISBN 0-02-860407-5 (pbk.)
    1. Zoo Animals. 2. Habitat (Ecology)
I. Challinor, David.   II. Title.   III. Series.
QL77.5.R62   1995
636.088'9—dc20   94-48288 CIP AC

Ligature Inc.

Publisher	**Series Design**	**Production**	**Editorial**
Jonathan P. Latimer	Patricia A. Eynon	Anne E. Spencer	Jean Knox
		Elizabeth Kun	Mary Ashford
			Steve Thomas

The Smithsonian Institution   **Macmillan**

Jessie Cohen   Mary Ann Lynch
                                         Laura C. Wood
                                         Robin Besofsky

Manufactured in Hong Kong
10 9 8 7 6 5 4 3 2 1

Contents

The New Zoo

In a rocky stream bed at a city zoo, two North American river otters chase one another, their back paws propelling them rapidly through the water. They seem unaware of the human visitors who press their noses against the glass display panel to get a better look. Otters are endangered species. Their natural river habitat is increasingly polluted and taken over for commercial development. Whether otters and other endangered species survive in the wild may depend in part on the public appeal of zoo exhibits like this one.

An otter retrieves fish from a pool in a zoo enclosure.

More than 100 million people visit zoos each year. This number exceeds attendance at all big-league baseball, football, and basketball games combined.

Zoos in Transformation

Welcome to the modern zoo, or wildlife conservation park, a multifaceted enterprise encompassing animal research and breeding, educational programs, and the daily care of hundreds of remarkable animals and plants. Gone are the iron bars and barren cages associated with zoos in the past. Here, aerial walkways, watery moats, and laminated security glass separate the animals from human visitors and from other animals. Large "immersion" exhibits that resemble wild habitats draw visitors inside the animals' environment.

Around the world, ambitious new exhibits such as these reflect a major change in the purpose and function of zoos. At the National Zoo in Washington, D.C., a 15,000-square-foot (4,560 sq m) exhibit called Amazonia contains 360 species of tropical plants, fish, birds, insects, amphibians, reptiles, and mammals. At the Arizona–Sonora Desert Museum near Tucson, Arizona, desert bighorn sheep graze among native plants in a mountain habitat sculpted from reinforced concrete. In a large, sprawling compound at the Minnesota Zoo, Siberian tigers prowl through the undergrowth, nearly hidden by tall grass.

Once a symbol of our ability to capture and confine wild animals, zoos today are links with the natural world. From their origins as private collections of exotic animals for the amusement of royalty, zoos have evolved into conservation centers and bioparks, where visitors see for themselves the importance of biodiversity and habitat preservation.

Once isolated in small, barred cages (below), gorillas at the National Zoo now live in family groups and move around freely (below right).

Carl Hagenbeck, a German animal dealer born in 1844, deserves credit for envisioning the first modern zoo. Though he began his career as an animal collector for menageries and circuses, Hagenbeck dreamed of creating a spacious zoological park where he might display animals in settings that resembled their natural habitats. His park opened in 1907 in Stellingen, Germany, and was a major engineering feat for its day. He removed all fences, bars, and other visible signs of confinement. For his African Plains exhibit, he displayed zebras, antelope, and gazelles grazing near lions, separated from them only by a deep, invisible moat.

Revolutionary in concept and expensive to execute, Hagenbeck's vision caught on slowly. Under the guidance of forward-thinking biologists and zoologists, zoos began to change. Animal behaviorists emphasized the importance of providing social contact for animals that are naturally social, such as monkeys, apes, elephants, and zebras. Research on animal mating and breeding habits, diet, and environmental adaptations led to a better understanding of animals. As animals were given outlets for instinctive behaviors and more space to move around, they became healthier, more active, and more interesting to zoo visitors.

Living in a re-creation of its tropical forest environment, an iguana (below) exhibits natural behavior, such as licking water from leaves. Although orangutans are normally solitary in the wild, they are social in zoos (bottom).

When humans cultivate and destroy wild habitats, such as the Amazon rain forest (top), animal populations suffer. There are about 300 golden lion tamarins (above) left in the forests of Brazil.

Over the past three decades, a more aware and demanding public has responded to the transformation of zoos. Media attention on endangered species such as elephants, mountain gorillas, and pandas has heightened public awareness. Television wildlife documentaries such as *Wild Kingdom*, which aired its first of 329 episodes in 1963, have educated a new generation of zoo visitors. People who have seen films of ostriches and wildebeests running in open grasslands object to seeing them in isolated pens. Furthermore, as inhabitants of an increasingly urban world, people want zoos to bring them closer to nature, to provide a sense of the wild.

Finally, and most urgently, zoos have changed because the habitats where animals live are in trouble. Wild, unspoiled lands are disappearing at an alarming rate, encroached upon and exploited by human development. With the loss of their habitats, animals are also disappearing. Only about 500 wild mountain gorillas remain in Zaire and Rwanda, Africa, their future made precarious by poachers, land-hungry farmers, and civil war. Black-footed ferrets are on the brink of extinction, their decline directly linked to the cultivation of the American plains and the decline of their prey animal, the prairie dog. As the human population grows, the wild areas of the globe diminish, and many animals may become extinct before scientists have even had a chance to identify them.

A Disappearing Act

Animal and plant species have always been vulnerable to extinction, as some species crowd out others or as food sources are depleted. The dinosaurs are the best known example, disappearing in a natural extinction that probably occurred approximately

65 million years ago. Between 1650 and 1850 it is estimated that an average of one species of plant or animal became extinct every five years. Today, as a result of human interference, the estimate is that 74 plant or animal species are becoming extinct every day. At this rate, 20 percent of the earth's species will be extinct within 30 years.

Zoos are doing more than just publicizing this environmental crisis. For more than a decade the American Zoo and Aquarium Association (AZA), which has 162 accredited North American zoos as members, has made conservation its primary goal. It administers a cooperative breeding and conservation program called the Species Survival Plans (SSPs), in which all major zoos participate.

A dual goal of SSPs is breeding selected species and reintroducing them to patrolled preserves. Already there are some success stories. The Asian wild horse, or Przewalski's horse, disappeared from the steppes of Mongolia in the 1970s but is being reintroduced today to protected grassland and desert habitats. Small numbers of zoo-bred golden lion tamarin monkeys are being released in protected regions of tropical forest in Brazil.

Instead of collecting wild animals, zoos now breed their own. Today, more than 90 percent of all mammals and 70 percent of all birds in North American zoos are born to zoo parents.

In all, SSPs are involved in breeding more than 50 endangered species, a tiny percentage of those threatened. Some of the breeding takes place in special facilities that are off-limits to the general public. For example, the National Zoo's Conservation and Research Center, one of three major off-exhibit breeding stations in the United States, covers 3,150 acres (7,900 ha) of rolling countryside in Front Royal, Virginia.

Places for Living Things

Because *habitat* plays such a key role in animal behavior and survival, it is helpful to know exactly what zoologists mean when they use the word. Simply put, a habitat is a specific place where a plant or animal lives. The habitat of an individual great blue heron might be a beaver pond in Minnesota, while the habitat of a camel might be an expanse of desert in Morocco. The living plant and animal organisms that share a common habitat and interact together form a *community*. The beaver pond community includes all of the pond's plants, fish, birds, mammals, invertebrates, and microscopic life. This pond community is also an *ecosystem,* a network of plants and animals interacting with their physical environment. An ecosystem can be relatively small, such as a beaver pond, or it may be a large, global ecological unit, such as a coniferous forest.

By standing on its hind legs, the gerenuk (left) can reach juicy foliage which enables it to live in dry habitats. The sapphire-spangled emerald hummingbird (right) uses its long bill to suck nectar from a flower.

The largest global ecosystems are called *biomes,* areas of the globe that contain similar plants and environmental conditions. Biomes include all living organisms, both plants and animals, as well as nonliving matter, such as rocks and soil. For example, tropical forests form a biome characterized by its proximity to the equator, high rainfall, and plant diversity. The ocean is a biome that includes everything from seaweed to microscopic plankton to blue whales. Within a biome there are many distinct habitats and communities. For example, the Mojave Desert, the Sahara Desert, and the Gobi Desert have unique characteristics and are geographically separate, but all are deserts and belong to the same biome.

Finding a Niche

Though animals in a biome may develop similar adaptations to help them survive, each species must develop its unique place in its habitat: its *niche*. A niche is the role played by an animal or plant in its environment. It may also refer to the place in the physical environment occupied by an organism. Where an animal lives, what it eats, and how it reproduces are all part of its niche. Each animal occupies a niche that is slightly different from that of other species in the same environment. It uses food sources that are not too heavily exploited by other animals and raises its young in territory that is not overcrowded. Over time, it evolves behaviors that allow it to coexist with other species.

The hoofed animals that graze on vegetation on the African savannas illustrate how niches work. Each animal has a distinct diet and feeds on a different part of the available vegetation, thus allowing all of the animals to coexist without depleting the plant resources. Zebras, which have strong teeth, eat coarse grasses, wildebeests eat long green stems, antelope eat the withered bottoms of stems, and giraffes reach above them to nibble on tree leaves.

As animals and plants gradually acquire a niche in a habitat, they sometimes develop a relationship with another species that helps one or both to survive. Any close relationship between two organisms of different species that benefits at least one of the two species is called *symbiosis*. For example, African birds called oxpeckers pick insects from the backs of rhinoceroses. In this case, both animals benefit from the relationship. The bird finds insects to eat, and the rhinoceros is freed from pests.

When collecting nectar, a bee performs a dual role (left). The bee brings the nectar back to the beehive and also tracks pollen from flower to flower, causing pollination. A giraffe's elongated neck and legs (right) allow it to feed on high leaves and avoid competition with other animals.

23

The Arizona–Sonora Desert Museum allows zoo visitors to see wildlife of the Arizona desert, such as the gila woodpecker (above).

Choices for the Future

With a few notable exceptions, zoos in the past were relatively similar, whereas it is likely that zoos in the future may be noted for the diversity of their exhibits. As local wild habitats shrink, small zoos may increasingly specialize in local wildlife. Large wildlife parks may also become more popular. Northwest Trek Wildlife Park near Tacoma, Washington, for example, features bison, moose, mountain goats, and other animals of the Northwest roaming freely over about 400 acres (162 ha) of woods, bogs, and meadowlands. Some large zoos may evolve into bioparks, where elements of existing zoos, aquariums, and natural history museums will combine to reflect the interdependence and diversity of all living things. Zoos in general will continue to play a vital role as wildlife conservation centers.

As zoos expand their role and image, the popular concept of "zoo animal" will also expand. Large mammals still make up 42 percent of the species exhibited, and visitors expect to see them, just as they also want to see rare and endangered animals. However, many small and equally fascinating animals, most of them requiring little exhibition space, are showing up in zoos. Bats, for example, are fascinating to zoo visitors, and make up about 20 percent of all species of mammals, yet they have been substantially underrepresented in zoos. The popularity of insect exhibits was discovered as early as 1978, when the Cincinnati Zoo opened the first insect house in the United States. Invertebrates—animals without backbones, which constitute 90

percent or more of terrestrial animal life—are joining the zoo population at such places as the new Invertebrate House at the National Zoo in Washington, D.C.

Whatever the zoo of the future may be like, one animal will continue to play a key role—the zoo visitor. Zoos have a vital interest in the people who walk through their gates. Only by knowing and understanding animals can people care about them. Each carefully planned exhibit aims to help visitors understand the complexity and vulnerability of the animal world.

The Barbary ape exhibit (above) at the National Zoo in Washington, D.C., simulates the apes' natural rocky habitat. At the National Zoo's Conservation and Research Center (below) endangered animals mate and rear offspring in a spacious and undisturbed environment.

Animals of the Tropical Forest

Near the equator, heavy rains and intense sunlight led to the creation of the tropical forest, the oldest and most complex terrestrial habitat on earth. Life thrives with such diversity and abundance in tropical forests that scientists believe they contain 90 percent of all plant and animal species. Only a small fraction of these species has been discovered and named, and few have been studied carefully.

Orangutans spend
most of their time
above the forest floor,
moving with dexterity
among the trees.

Layers of the Tropical Forest

Fruit-eating bat

Two-toed sloth

Scarlet macaw

Tokay gecko

Iguana

Chimpanzees

Gorilla

Leaf-cutter ants

Tropical forests contain several layers, or stories, of foliage. Each has its own characteristics and inhabitants. The highest layer is the upper canopy, made up of the crowns of the tallest trees.

The canopy provides an airy, sunny habitat, with isolated emergent trees soaring to 200 feet (60 m). In these tall trees live fly-ing and climbing animals such as eagles, macaws, monkeys, sloths and invertebrate organisms.

Below the canopy is a less dense layer of foliage called the understory, or lower canopy. It is formed by young trees strug-gling toward the sun and by mature semi-shade-tolerant trees. The lower canopy

Emergent trees

Harpy eagle

Black spider monkey

Red howler monkey

Canopy

Lower canopy

Blue poison-arrow frog

Emerald tree boa

Forest floor

Jaguar

plays host to mammals ranging in size from squirrels to chimpanzees and to reptiles such as emerald tree boas and vipers.

Many animals, including bats and sloths, move between the upper and lower canopies. Below the understory are seedlings and shade-tolerant shrubs.

The surface of the lowest layer of the for- est, the forest floor, is covered with a rela- tively thin layer of fallen leaves and rapidly decaying debris. Although insects are found at every level, millions of them, from ants to beetles, live on the forest floor. Although some large carnivores such as jaguars and leopards spend time in trees, they generally descend to the forest floor to hunt.

Like all macaws, the blue-and-yellow macaw lives in the tropical forests of the Amazon basin. The collecting of macaws for sale as pets threatens their population in the wild.

An Abundance of Life

Take a walk through one of the world's tropical forests. Trees tower overhead, blocking the sunlight with their leafy crowns. In the deep shade below, young saplings and palms struggle toward the light, and insects swarm. Water from a recent rainshower drips from the leaves. Vines, exotic orchids, mosses, and ferns—many growing directly on top of one another—drape the branches of massive tree trunks.

You will hear the animals before you see them: the shrieks of monkeys, the chatter of birds. Some animals, such as macaws and birds of paradise, are bright and conspicuous among the trees. Others, including some species of insects and snakes, are camouflaged against the lush vegetation.

Many animals in tropical forests never descend to the ground, living their entire lives in the treetops. Using the rope-climbing techniques of mountaineers, scientists today are scaling the leafy heights of the tropical-forest canopy to study these animals and penetrate the mysteries of their ancient habitat.

Tropical Forests

Tropical forests are found in Central and South America, Africa, Southeast Asia, Australia and the islands of the Pacific. The largest tropical forest in the world surrounds the Amazon River in northwestern Brazil and neighboring countries, covering an area almost the size of the United States.

Life in a Bromeliad

Bromeliad is the common name for the pineapple family of herbs, small shrubs, and Spanish moss, found in American tropical forests. Most bromeliads grow on trees or on other plants. Bromeliads take in moisture directly from the air and from water that runs down trunks and branches.

Typical bromeliads have straplike leaves that cluster snugly together at their base, forming a watertight cup around the plant's stem. Rainwater collects in this cup, forming a reservoir that helps the plant survive during dry spells.

Bromeliads can hold as little as a cupful of water or many gallons. Dead insects and decaying forest debris accumulate in the water and provide nutrients for the

Bromeliads are also useful sources of water for treetop animals. A passing lizard or monkey may stop to drink there. Mosquitoes lay their eggs in water stored in the bromeliad leaves. Ants often nest in the stem, preying on insects attracted by the water.

Poison-arrow frogs are unusual bromeliad visitors. They shield their eggs from predators by depositing them under damp leaves on the forest floor. When the tadpoles hatch, certain species carry the tadpoles on their backs into the upper branches of trees, where they deposit each tadpole within its own bromeliad, slipping it into the reservoir of water. Some species of poison-arrow frogs even revisit the bromeliads and lay infertile eggs, which

The National Zoo's Amazonia exhibit re-creates the lush plant life of the Amazon rainforest.

Strangler Fig

One common tropical plant, the strangler fig, begins life as a seed, taking root in the branches of a canopy tree. At first it lives as an epiphyte, drawing nutrients from rainwater. As it grows, it sends branches skyward and roots down to the ground. Over time, its spiraling roots gradually smother the tree it grows on. Eventually the host tree dies and rots, and the strangler fig remains as a free-standing tree. Mature strangler figs are sometimes among the largest trees in the forest, their sweet fruit and sheltering roots attracting countless animals, birds, and insects.

Animals of the Canopy

The canopy is the heart of all tropical forests, where life flourishes in abundance. Here, with access to plenty of light and rain, trees flower and bear fruit, drawing chattering swarms of monkeys, parrots, and other fruit-and-leaf eaters. Here, too, plants called epiphytes, including ferns, orchids, and mosses, grow on other plants. Without access to soil or groundwater, epiphytes absorb nutrients from rain, dust particles, and tiny bits of animal matter. Bromeliads, which are cup-shaped epiphytes, are among the most successful and numerous of these water collectors. Epiphytes grow so well in this aerial habitat that some trees grow tiny roots into the epiphytes that cover them. The weight of the epiphytes in a single tree may reach several tons. (See "Life in a Bromeliad" on p. 31.)

Monkeys and Apes

Humans, apes, and monkeys are all mammals belonging to the *primate order*. Primate characteristics include binocular eyesight, and the centrality of a social group. Tropical forest primates include monkeys, apes, lemurs, tarsiers, marmosets and tamarins.

Traveling in their airy habitat in search of food, monkeys move with ease through the canopy. Some monkeys swing by their arms from tree to tree, their flexible shoulder joints making a half-turn with each forward swing, a means of locomotion called *brachiation*. Brachiators have elongated fingers that can grip and release branches quickly. Other monkeys, usually smaller primates with lighter bodies and long legs, move by leaping. For added balance, most monkeys of the Americas have

prehensile tails, meaning tails that can grip vines and branches. (See "Prehensile Tails" on p. 34.)

As a further adaptation, primates have three-dimensional or *stereoscopic vision*, which helps them judge distances correctly as they swing and leap from branch to branch. As in humans, this eye placement makes room for a larger brain but reduces the muzzle space needed for a good sense of smell.

Spider Monkeys Spider monkeys are among the most agile primates of the tropical forests of Central and South America. Primarily fruit eaters, spider monkeys also eat leaves, seeds, insects, and birds' eggs. They forage alone or in small groups, but when they find a rich food source, such as a ripe fig tree, they may gather in groups of 20 to 30. They are noisy animals, calling out to one another with a cry like a horse's whinny. Their cry makes them easy prey for hunters, and local people sometimes kill them for food. Spider monkeys seldom descend to the forest floor, where they are likely to encounter terrestrial predators. Canopy predators include hawks and eagles.

Woolly Monkeys Woolly monkeys also make good use of a prehensile tail. They are fruit-and-leaf eaters and rarely descend to the ground. Their fur is longer and thicker than that of spider monkeys, with whom they often compete for the same food and space. The **muriqui monkey,** although closely related to spider monkeys, is more like a woolly monkey in appearance.

The black spider monkey (left) is the only spider monkey with a completely black coat. All the others have dark fur with patches of white, gold, yellow, or brown. The woolly monkey (right) lives in the tropical forests of Colombia and Brazil.

Prehensile Tails

Some animals native to the Americas, such as monkeys and opossums, have a long tail adapted for life in the trees. The muscular tail of the monkey is bare on the underside for about a quarter of the length from the tip.

Monkeys use their tail as a fifth limb for grasping and suspension. A prehensile tail frees their arms and legs for swinging from branch to branch in the treetops. Howler, spider, and woolly monkeys can suspend their full body weight from their tail while they eat.

African monkeys do not have a prehensile tail. The great apes have no tail at all. Scientists theorize that a prehensile tail may have evolved in some primates to extend their reach to buds, blossoms, or fruit growing at branch ends. Primates with this ability could thereby compete with bats and birds for this rich food source.

Baby squirrel monkeys, such as the one above, are often looked after by older females without young of their own. These females help the mother by providing extra care and protection. The Bolivian red howler monkey (right) is an example of successful zoo breeding. Twenty-four red howlers have been born at the San Diego Zoo since 1981.

Squirrel Monkeys Named for their small size, squirrel monkeys of South America lack a prehensile tail. They mark their territory by wiping their tail, coated with their own urine, on tree trunks and branches. Eighty percent of their diet is fruit, primarily figs, which are the most common forest fruit. When necessary they can exist for a time on insects.

Howler Monkeys The noisiest monkeys of South America are howler monkeys. The penetrating, territorial calls of male howlers resound through the trees, especially at dawn, and can be heard almost 2 miles (3.2 km) away. Their extraordinary call is produced by air passing over a bone in their larynx, somewhat like air blown across the narrow opening of a bottle. Since most howler monkeys range widely, they use their calls to announce a temporary claim to a particular territory. Like other monkeys, howlers live in social groups called troops, some troops having as many as 45 members. All six species of howlers are exclusively herbivores, meaning they feed on plants, especially leaves.

Gibbons Gibbons are apes inhabiting Southeast Asian tropical forests. Though as loud as howler monkeys', gibbons' calls are much more melodious and higher pitched. Males and females call in duets, the more practiced duets belonging to couples that have been together for some time. Included in their exchange of calls is the female's "great call," which announces to nearby females that her mate is spoken for.

Expert brachiators, gibbons are the most acrobatic of all the apes, propelling themselves up to 30 feet (9.1 m) with one swing. They sleep and forage in tall emergent trees. Like monkeys, if they miss a branch they do not panic, but plummet calmly through the air, looking for another branch to grab. They cannot always break their fall, however, and many gibbons studied in the wild have bone fractures that have healed.

Gibbons live in small family groups of two parents and two to four offspring. They have fixed territories, which range from 50 to 225 acres (20–90 ha).

Like gorillas, gibbons are afraid of water. Their zoo enclosures are often separated by moats rather than by walls or bars.

A siamang (top), the largest of the gibbons, skillfully climbs in an emergent tree. Suspended by one arm, gibbons (center) reach for ripe fruit located on the ends of branches. Gibbon babies, like this common gibbon (right), stay close to their mothers until they are a year old.

As they mature, male orangutans develop fleshy cheeks and large, inflatable throat sacs. During territorial confrontations with other males, orangutans show aggression by inflating and calling from their throat sacs.

Orangutan Movement through the trees is a tricky business for orangutans, another ape that lives on the islands of Sumatra and Borneo off the southeast coast of Asia. Unusually large for canopy animals, orangutan males in the wild may reach 200 pounds (91 kg), and females may weigh 110 pounds (50 kg). They move cautiously, distributing their weight evenly between their hands and feet, choosing branches that will hold them.

Orangutans prepare for sleep by building a large platform nest of branches each night high in the treetops. They shelter from rain and sun by holding leafy branches over their heads like umbrellas. Males normally spend their time alone, but females may temporarily band together. In zoos, orangutans are often quite sociable.

Orangutans are among the few creatures in the animal kingdom that use tools. They use sticks to dig termites out of termite mounds, stones to crack nuts, and leaves to soak up drinking water or to clean themselves. Here, an orangutan uses a stick to dig for honey that has been placed in a mound by zookeepers.

Female black lemurs (left) have reddish-brown fur and white ear tufts. Only the males are black. Red-ruffed lemur females (above right) usually give birth to twins. They are the only lemurs to leave their young alone while foraging for food.

Ring-tailed lemurs are highly sociable animals and reproduce successfully in zoos if housed in family groups of five or six.

Two Primate Ancestors

Millions of years ago, Madagascar and Comoros were part of the mainland of Africa, but a geological rift turned them into separate islands. They provided a haven for lemurs, which, over time, disappeared on the mainland. Today only a small fraction of the tropical forests in these regions remain, and lemurs, ancestors of today's primates, are again becoming extinct.

Lemurs A thick fur coat, large, staring eyes, and a foxlike muzzle are distinguishing marks of lemurs. Some have long, bushy tails. All are tree dwellers and eat fruit, flowers, and leaves. Ridged pads on the soles of their feet help them walk on horizontal branches from tree to tree. They also make short leaps on their long hind legs. When on the ground, they walk on all four feet or hop on their hind legs.

The Jungle: Myth or Reality?

The jungle of Hollywood's Tarzan films is largely a myth. Leopards and gorillas do not stalk and devour human visitors. Most animals avoid human contact, and the chances of meeting a large predator are remote.

However, goliath beetles, carnivorous bats, and bird-eating spiders (above) do live in tropical forests. Massive vines dangle from overhanging branches. Animals and plants assume such diverse shapes, sizes, colors, and behaviors that they sometimes seem to have evolved from the creative mind of a film director.

Tarsiers Another group of unusual-looking primates lives on the islands of Borneo, Sumatra, and Sulawesi in Southwest Asia. Tarsiers are tiny creatures only 3½ to 6 inches high (9–15 cm), not including a long, hairless tail. Found in dense jungle vegetation, they are primarily nocturnal, sleeping during the day by clinging to a vertical branch. Like other primates, tarsiers have binocular vision. Their large eyes have little room for movement, but they can rotate their heads almost full circle.

Excellent leapers, tarsiers can easily jump more than six feet (2 m), clinging to branches with the help of rounded pads on their fingers and toes. They forage for insects by directing their ears toward insect sounds in nearby foliage, then leaping forward and trapping the prey in both hands. Baby tarsiers, born with their eyes open, can leap when only about a month old.

Philippine tarsiers (above) have soft fur, long toes, and large hind legs. They also have razor-sharp teeth for eating beetles and scorpions. Zoos must provide tarsiers with live insects to eat or the animals will die.

A Grip Like a Sloth

A sloth's habit of hanging upside down is also a bid to conserve energy. Because its claws lock shut, it takes less energy for a sloth to hang from a branch than for an animal of the same size to balance on top of a branch. Its grip is so strong that a dead sloth may remain hanging from a branch until its body decomposes.

Upside Down in the Canopy

Sloths Common to the Americas, two-toed sloths are mammals that live in both the upper and lower canopy. They weigh up to about 17 pounds (8 kg). Since sloths spend most of their lives upside down, eating, sleeping, mating, and even giving birth in this position, the hair on their bodies divides along their abdomen and falls toward their backs, allowing rainwater to drip off easily. They may spend up to 18 hours hardly changing their position except to move their jaws and grasp leaves.

Sloths' faces, like those of the two-toed sloths below, are flat. Their facial features are somewhat hidden by their fur, which often is tinged green with algae.

The staple of a sloth's diet is leaves, which are difficult to digest. Sloths have an especially slow digestive process. The bacteria in their stomachs must be warm enough to break down the leaves. Therefore, each morning a sloth must raise its body temperature by finding an open tree in which to sun itself. It takes a sloth up to one hundred hours to digest one stomachful of food. A sloth may starve if there are too many cool, cloudy days in a row, thus preventing its stomach bacteria from functioning properly.

Sloths slowly descend to the forest floor about once a week to defecate, depositing small, hard feces near the base of the tree in which they live. (Monkeys,

Newborn sloths are cradled on their mother's belly, but begin to practice hanging upside down at about 20 to 25 days old.

by contrast, defecate freely from the treetops.) This laborious trip may conceal the sloth's presence in the tree, or even have nutritional benefit for the tree whose leaves the sloth consumes.

Bats, like the hammer-headed bat (above left), fold their wings over their bodies when resting. Fruit bats (above right) use their clawed thumbs to grip fruit and move it into their mouths.

Bats Found in every part of the world except Antarctica and the Arctic, bats make up one fourth of all mammal species. They originated in tropical forests, where they inhabit both the upper and lower canopy. Bats make up half of all mammal species found in tropical forests.

Like all bats, tropical bats rest hanging upside down by their clawed feet in trees or caves, or under rocks and large leaves. Many bats are insect eaters. Others sip nectar from flowers, and still others are fruit eaters. Some bats catch birds, lizards, frogs, or even fish.

Insect-eating bats utilize specialized, highly developed *echolocation*. By emitting a rapid series of ultrasonic sounds, possibly as many as 200 per second, they can locate obstacles and flying insects. Fruit- and nectar-eating bats have less developed echolocation systems. Instead they rely on their large eyes and good night vision.

False vampire bats of Africa, Asia, and Australia are large and carnivorous with a wingspan of almost 3 feet (1 m). The floor of the hollow tree where they nest is often covered with the blood and bones of their prey. This refuse becomes a source of nutrients for insects and for the tree itself.

Vampire bats, with a wingspan of about 12 inches (30 cm), are smaller than false vampire bats. The **common vampire bat** has adapted to both arid and humid tropical regions, but has a limited diet. It feeds only on the blood of large mammals, mostly livestock such as cattle or horses. It stalks its sleeping prey by flying close to the ground. With sharp, highly specialized teeth it makes a shallow bite in its prey and then laps up blood until it is almost too heavy to fly. Anticoagulants in the bat's saliva ensure that the blood will not clot until the bat has finished its meal. The vampire bat's bite is not fatal, but the bat often carries rabies and thus endangers the life of its prey.

The common vampire bat (above) uses its toe claws to hang upside down.

Zoo Breeding and Endangered Animals

Sumatran tiger

Grevy's zebra foal

As the number of animals on the list of endangered species grows, zoos are increasingly dedicated to the complex task of saving species through breeding wild animals. These programs help pass on healthy genes to the next generation of animals. Genes are the basic code of heredity contained within

When scientists try to breed endangered animals from among the small population of a single zoo, inbreeding is likely to occur. Inbred animals are closely related and their genes are too similar. They often suffer from infertility and are less resistant to disease.

Zoos keep detailed computer records on

Golden lion tamarins

Komodo dragon hatching

Malayan tapir baby

A central computer system called the International Species Inventory System (ISIS) arranges genetically diverse matches from different zoos, even if this means flying in a Sumatran tiger from a zoo in Southeast Asia to mate with a female of the same species in Washington, D.C.

All major zoos in both the United States and abroad participate in the Species Survival Plans (SSPs). The SSPs coordinate breeding efforts for more than 50 species of animals urgently in need of help. The list includes cheetahs, rhinoceroses, Asian elephants, orangutans, pandas, and Puerto Rican crested toads. The long-range goal of the SSPs is to build up large enough populations so that these animals can be returned to their natural habitats.

Animals of the Lower Canopy

In the lower canopy live apes and monkeys, sloths, lizards, bats, and many species of birds. Food resources are abundant and include small animals, birds' eggs, buds, seeds, fruits, and palms. The luxuriant plant growth of the lower canopy is rich in nutrients, and if unharmed by outside influence, it easily supports the animal population.

Chimpanzees Chimpanzees are classified not as monkeys but as one of the great apes, along with gorillas and orangutans. Chimpanzees live in both the rain forests and the grasslands of central Africa. They are far less adapted to life in the trees than the monkeys of the upper canopy. When chimpanzees have to travel any distance, they do so on the ground, walking half-erect on the soles of their feet and balancing on the knuckles of their hands. Their arms are long, and their reach from hand to hand is twice as great as their height.

Like many other lower-canopy plants, the rainbow heliconia's seeds lie dormant in the ground until a tree falls and sunlight reaches the forest floor. In this light the seeds sprout and grow.

Baby chimpanzees are carried by their mothers for the first five months of life, or until they are strong enough to ride on her back.

Ninety percent of a chimpanzee's diet is fruits and vegetables, although they also eat insects, eggs, birds, lizards, and small mammals. They travel considerable distances to satisfy their love for fruit. When a chimpanzee finds a tree with ripe fruit, it will hoot loudly to its companions or drum on the roots of the tree. Chimpanzees usually travel in family groups or in small troops of unrelated adults. Occasionally, chimpanzees hunt cooperatively and then share the meal. They may, however, turn against and kill other chimpanzees that wander onto their territory.

Chimpanzees' opposable thumbs maneuver food and objects easily. Family groups (below) change often in number, age range, and gender ratio.

What to look for

To get the attention of females, male chimpanzees shake tree branches.

Chimps sometimes forage for food that zookeepers hide in the crevices of trees and rocks.

Chimps and other apes have very large hairless ears.

To rest, an emerald
tree boa (above) balances
on a tree limb. It grasps
a branch (below) with its
tail and hangs its coils
evenly on each side.

Snakes

Like bats, snakes are found in every part of the world except the polar regions. Many tropical forest snakes are related to snakes of tropical grasslands; many have green coloring that provides camouflage in the forest. Active in the early morning and evening, most tropical snakes are not strictly nocturnal. Only a small percentage of the many species are venomous.

Boa constrictors Boa constrictors live in both forests and grasslands. Small boas, such as the **emerald tree boa** of the Amazon River basin, forage in trees, while larger ones spend most of their time on the ground. Like all snakes, boas are carnivores and eat a variety of mammals and birds. Their bite is painful but nonvenomous. Boas coil themselves around prey and smother the animal before swallowing it.

Green mambas Poisonous green mambas, which grow up to 9 feet (2.7 m) long, are found in central and southern African forests. They spend the hot part of the day basking, often in

Eyelash vipers (left), like all vipers, squeeze venom through their fangs and into their prey. This action requires well-developed muscles. These muscles, combined with venom glands, give vipers a characteristically wide, triangular head.

groups of three or more, camouflaged among the leaves of the upper canopy. **Black mambas,** the largest venomous snakes in Africa, are found in more open country. They grow up to 14 feet (4.3 m) long, and their strike is deadly.

Vipers Lance-headed vipers of South American forests have distinctive, sometimes brilliant, markings. The **eyelash viper,** measuring up to 2 feet long (.6 m), preys upon frogs and lizards. Its venom is toxic but, like that of the boa, its bite is rarely life–threatening. The eyelash viper is an excellent tree climber.

Several species of **fer-de-lance,** poisonous snakes ranging up to 8 feet (2.5 m) in length, are found throughout Central and South America. Their highly potent venom destroys tissues and causes internal bleeding. In general, those living among branches are green; those on the forest floor are blotchy-brown to camouflage them when they coil in leaf litter to ambush prey.

The Green mamba (above) is in the first stages of shedding its skin. Reptiles periodically shed their outer skin layer. A new skin layer replaces the older, worn-out one and allows room for growth.

The green iguana, like the Amazon species shown here, has a crest of scales that runs the entire length of its body, from the neck to the tip of the tail. It is a rapid and agile tree climber.

Lizards

Lizards are possibly the best known *reptiles*—cold-blooded animals, or *ectotherms*, whose temperature changes with that of their environment. All lizards have sensitive, extendable tongues, which they use for detecting food, sensing the proximity of predators, or picking up the scent of a possible mate. Like snakes, they either lay eggs or give birth to live young.

Iguanas Many species of terrestrial and tree-dwelling iguanas inhabit Central and South America. The **green iguana,** also known as the **South American iguana,** has ridged feet for climbing trees. It is the largest iguana, measuring up to six and a half feet (2 m). Iguanas can defend themselves by biting aggressors or lashing out with their tails. Most iguanas lay eggs, leaving as many as 40 eggs in a hole.

Geckos Over six hundred known species of geckos are found in tropical climates. Geckos are insect-eating lizards with a *regenerative* tail. Like many lizards, geckos, if seized, can shed their tail and then grow another. Like iguanas, geckos have ridged feet. Walking upside down, they easily scale vertical surfaces. Geckos remain camouflaged and motionless in the face of danger.

Tokay geckos communicate with a variety of sounds ranging from chirps to clicks. Their unique "to-kay" call gives them their name. Tokay geckos live in southern Asia.

Chameleons have binocular vision—both their eyes can focus on the same object. Each eye can rotate independently, so they can look forward with one eye and sideways with the other.

Chameleons Chameleons can change their color in response to heat, light, or threats from predators. They probably do not, as is commonly believed, change color to blend with the colors and patterns of their environment. Like parrots, chameleons have *zygodactyl* feet—two in front and two behind. They also have prehensile tails, as do many other animals in tropical forests. Though their common food sources are insects and spiders, some larger chameleons eat birds and small mammals.

Frogs and Toads

The more than 2,600 species of frogs and toads form the largest group of *amphibians.* Like reptiles, amphibians are cold-blooded animals, but they have smooth, moist skin instead of scales. All frogs and toads can excrete mucus from special glands in their skin. In most species this mucus is not harmful. Notable exceptions are poison-arrow frogs and marine toads of the tropical forests of Central and South America.

Poison-arrow frogs Small, and often brightly colored to warn predators, some species of poison-arrow frogs contain a toxin so potent that many South American Indians use it to poison the tips of their blow pipe darts. The frogs are aggressive not only with other frog species but also within their own groups.

Marine toads The largest of all toads, marine toads cause extreme pain and even death to predators by squirting toxic secretions from glands behind the head.

The blue (above) and green (below) poison-arrow frogs are among the 116 poison-arrow species. Some are near extinction.

Big Cats in the Lower Canopy and on the Forest Floor

Many predatory cats are found in both tropical forest and grassland habitats (see also Chapter 3). Exceptional features of adaptation, such as powerful jaws, speed, and stealth, have helped them survive. Big cats are carnivores and feed at the top of the tropical-forest *food chain*. A food chain is the passing of energy from one organism to another in an ecosystem.

Big cats rely on their excellent hearing and eyesight when hunting. Like house cats, their eyes can adapt to day and night vision. Their coats provide excellent camouflage. All of the big cats of the tropical forest are threatened by deforestation and agricultural encroachment. The rare **clouded leopard** of India and Southeast Asia, which hides in the branches of trees before pouncing on prey, is especially endangered.

The clouded leopard's coat has light brown, black-rimmed markings that provide excellent camouflage in the dappled shade of the tropical forest. Clouded leopards are born with completely black markings.

Jaguar Jaguars are closely related to leopards, and at first glance the species look very much alike. Like leopards, jaguars have a yellowish undercoat covered with black spots. However, jaguars are somewhat bigger, more compact, and have a slightly larger head. They are solitary, territorial, and aggressive toward other jaguars.

In isolated regions of the Amazon rain forest, jaguars hunt by day, but in more populated regions they have taken to hunting at night. Like leopards, they spend much of their time in trees but hunt mostly on the ground. They are excellent swimmers and often live near fresh water. Their prey includes wild pigs, tapirs, monkeys, reptiles, and fish. Today jaguars have been hunted nearly to extinction in much of Central and South America.

Jaguars grunt while hunting and growl when frightened or threatened. Male jaguars mew softly during the mating season. Unlike lions, jaguars never roar.

Jaguar

The name *jaguar* comes from a word that means "it kills with a bound" in the language of people of the Amazon region. The name is accurate, since jaguars often manage to kill their prey at the first leap. If they jump from an overhanging branch, the impact usually breaks the prey animal's back.

Tigers Tigers are found in India, China, and Southeast Asia. Adult male Indian tigers weigh up to 570 pounds (260 kg). Adult male Sumatran tigers are smaller, weighing up to about 380 pounds (180 kg). Tigers have adapted to a range of habitats, including tropical forests, evergreen forests, grasslands, and rocky country, and are primarily ground dwellers.

Like other big cats, tigers mark the boundaries of their territory with urine and hunt in that area alone, preying on large mammals, such as wild pigs, deer, and bison, roaring when they have made a kill. Following a gestation period of about three and a half months, females have two or three cubs, but sometimes as many as six. Tigers may live as long as 26 years.

Although tigers seldom attack human beings, those that do are a serious threat. In India, about three dozen people are reported killed and eaten by tigers each year. Because of their perceived threat to humans, and because of their beautiful coats, tigers have been hunted relentlessly over the past two centuries. In 1920 there were an estimated 100,000 tigers in the wild; by the 1970s the number had dropped to 4,000. As a result of efforts by zoos and other conservation organizations, the worldwide tiger population had increased to about 8,000 by the mid-1990s.

Like jaguars, tigers often live near water. They have been known to swim as far as 18 miles (29 km).

The white bengal tiger (below) is a rare mutation, with a white coat, black stripes, and blue eyes.

Animals of the Forest Floor

On the lowest layer, the forest floor, the air is still. It is hotter than the lower canopy and even more humid. Animals found at this level include ocelots, mandrill baboons, and many species of ants and beetles. Few plants grow in the deep shade. Unlike the forests of North America, where cool temperatures slow the rate of decay, tropical forests have no rich layer of decaying vegetation. Dead leaves, animal dung, and other forest litter are quickly broken down by fungi and insects, leaving few nutrients for plant growth.

In adaptation to the surface soil layer, which contains what nutrients are available, trees found in tropical forests have evolved shallow roots and thin rootlets to absorb water and minerals as efficiently as possible. Because their roots are not deep enough to anchor them firmly, some tree species, as they reach maturity, produce large supporting projections called buttresses.

The presence of large predators such as big cats makes the tropical forest floor a dangerous place for prey animals. Deer, antelope, rodents, and other animals are wary and easily frightened, dashing away at the slightest sound. Because of sparse ground vegetation in dense forest, most animals of the lowest forest layer inhabit clearings or areas of newer undergrowth along riverbanks.

Leaf-cutter ants eat fungi that grow on the leaves they collect. This dietary adaptation helps the ants survive on the forest floor.

The male mandrill baboon (left), is much larger than the female mandrill (right). All mandrills have red muzzles, but only males have blue ridges on the sides. The male's special coloring and large size may attract females.

At the San Diego Zoo, young trees create a shaded habitat for okapi. Because okapi nibble tree bark, the trunks are covered with protective cuffs.

Browsers on the Tropical Forest Floor

Okapi One of the rarest animals in the African tropical forest is the okapi, a hoofed animal related to giraffes. Okapi are about 5 feet tall (1.5 m) at the shoulder, and their neck is slightly longer than that of a horse. Their coat is deep purplish-black, with black-and-white stripes on the haunches and front legs. With their remarkable long tongue, okapi can pluck leaves, buds, and small branches from saplings. They can even clean their eyes with their tongue. By stretching their neck and hind legs they can browse on low-hanging branches. They spend their time alone, in pairs, or in small family groups. The forest–dwelling people in Zaire have always hunted the okapi, but western naturalists did not learn of the okapi's existence until 1900. Under the Species Survival Plans, their breeding is coordinated by Illinois' Brookfield Zoo, which is run by the Chicago Zoological Society.

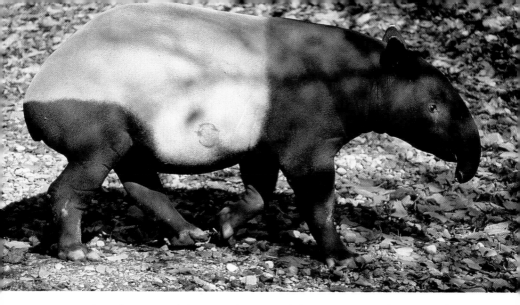

Tapir Found in the tropical forests of Asia and the Americas, tapir are stocky animals, 2¹/₂ to 4 feet tall (.8 to 1.2 m) at the shoulder, with short, bristly hair and a tapered snout. Like rhinoceroses, they have five toes. In common with okapi, tapir are solitary animals, living on leaves, buds, and twigs. Tapir usually sleep in the forest during the day and venture into nearby grassy or shrub areas to feed at night. They live near water and are strong swimmers. The striped and spotted coloring of newborn tapir camouflages them against the forest floor.

One species, **Baird's tapir**, the largest plant eater in the tropical forests of the Americas, has evolved an interesting defense against the many toxic plants found in the rain forest. It eats a little of each of a wide variety of plants, but never too much of any single plant. Its body can tolerate small amounts of various toxins so long as it does not have to absorb a large dose.

Peccaries Large mammals, peccaries are found in the tropical forests of Central and South America. They are wild pigs with a thick neck, slender legs, small hooves, and a coarse and bristly coat. Peccaries forage during cooler hours and at night for fruit, berries, roots, bulbs, and occasional insects. They have strong jaw muscles and have evolved an excellent sense of smell to detect bulbs underground.

Fast runners, peccaries are preyed on by big cats such as jaguars. Baby peccaries can run just a few hours after birth. Depending on their species, peccaries live in small herds of ten or in large herds with as many as one hundred members.

Dark patches on the head and rear of the Malayan tapir break up its body outline, confusing potential attackers. Tapir have streamlined bodies to help them maneuver easily in dense undergrowth.

Collared peccaries live in groups of 15 to 50. When attacked by predators, peccaries scatter and run in all directions. Sometimes one peccary will confront the predator, allowing the others to escape.

In the wild, 40 percent of gorilla babies die before they are three years old. About one-fourth of these infants are killed by male gorillas other than the infants' fathers. Gorillas born in zoos have an 80 percent rate of survival.

The Largest Herbivores

Gorillas and elephants, two of the biggest and most intimidating animals of the tropical forest, live almost entirely on vegetation. Oddly enough, some bigger animals tend to have slower metabolisms and therefore can make do with the relatively modest supply of energy provided by an entirely vegetarian diet.

Gorillas Gorillas usually live in forests or on open mountainsides where there is plenty of vegetation at ground level. Found primarily in central Africa, their total population is estimated to be less than 50,000. They spend as much as half the day feeding on favorite plants such as wild celery, thistles, bamboo shoots, and ferns, carefully avoiding toxic plants. They eat a small amount of fruit and never eat meat in the wild.

Adult male gorillas weigh 350 to 400 pounds (160 to 180 kg) —females are about half that size—so their tree climbing must be done very cautiously. Like orangutans, they use branches and leaves to build nests for sleeping. In some regions gorillas build

With hands very similar to human hands, gorillas grasp and move objects with ease.

these nests in trees; in other regions, on the ground. They cannot swim and even dislike wading, which is why a moat is usually sufficient to keep a zoo gorilla in its enclosure.

Gorillas are highly social animals, living in groups of two to twenty members, led by a dominant male. The dominant male organizes the movements of his group and protects its members, especially the females with young infants, who stay closest to him. The group is an extended harem, the leader usually mating with all of the females except his daughters.

A mature male gorilla is called a silverback because of the gray fur on his back and sides. This gray patch begins to appear when the male gorilla is twelve years old; rather than a sign of old age, it indicates that he is entering his prime. Silverbacks occasionally have fierce fights with one another over their right to dominate a group.

If a gorilla feels threatened, it may begin screaming, pounding its chest, and tearing up saplings and foliage. These displays are primarily threats. Gorillas do not normally attack people unless they feel that they are in danger or unless the intruder panics and runs away. Most gorillas are shy and peaceable creatures, seeming most content when left undisturbed.

Gorillas have small ears and a wide nose with large nostrils (above right). Male gorillas, like the lowland silverback (above left), have a large, bony crest at the back of their skull. All gorillas have strong jaw muscles needed for chewing large amounts of food.

The Peacock

In the wild, peacocks live in the tropical forests of the Indian subcontinent and of the nation of Sri Lanka. The name peacock is often used to refer to the entire common peafowl species but it accurately describes only the male bird. Females are called peahens. They are members of the pheasant family of birds.

Although usually found at ground level, peafowl have powerful wings and can roost in the highest branches of deciduous trees. They live in small flocks and feed on seeds, plants, and even small mammals such as mice.

Like other male pheasants, peacocks have evolved elaborate plumage to attract females. The common, or blue, peacock has ers. These plumes are the upper tail covers Each feather has a colorful, iridescent de sign that looks very much like an eye. Only males have the train, which is often mis taken for a tail.

During the mating season, males stake out a territory where they attract and mate with a flock of peahens. They raise thei feathers into a spectacular half-circle display and emit a loud call. The male performs a complicated dance around each female by fanning its train and shaking it feathers, causing a rustling sound. The sight and sound of the colorful moving feathers entice the hens to mate. After mating, the hens return to shallow nest they have made in the forest's thorny un

Birds of the Tropical Forest

Parrots Even in the relatively open spaces of the upper canopy, birds are easily hidden by foliage. Most tropical-forest parrots are predominantly green, making them nearly invisible in their leafy habitat. Some parrots, however, such as **South American macaws,** have brilliant plumage.

The blue-crowned hanging parrot (above left) has a special tip on its tongue that allows it to brush nectar and seeds from flowers. The red-collared lorikeet (above) is a brightly colored and noisy parrot. The blue-and-yellow macaw's tail sometimes grows to two-thirds of its body length (below).

Most parrots rely on a wide range of calls to keep in touch with one another. Although some parrot species have an uncanny ability to mimic sounds, especially human speech, parrots in the wild do not imitate the songs of other birds. It is not uncommon for parrots to live 30 years or more in the wild, and some have lived for 80 years in zoos.

Large parrots are not fast fliers—with the exception of macaws, which are notably swift for heavy parrots. Although most parrots can fly strongly and well, tree-dwelling parrots climb, rather than fly, from branch to branch to get seeds and fruit. They use their bill to help them climb, clamping it to a branch as they grasp another branch with their feet. Parrots have zygodactyl feet—two outer toes pointing forward and two middle toes pointing backward. This characteristic gives them greater dexterity than most other birds, allowing them both to grip food and to bring it to their bill.

Smaller, often brilliantly plumed species of parrots, such as **lories** and **lorikeets,** live on pollen and nectar from flowering trees and shrubs. Other smaller parrots, such as **parakeets,** often eat seeds on or near the ground.

What to look for

Parrots are either left- or right-footed. Each parrot favors the use of one foot for gripping and eating.

Adults have brighter plumage than young parrots.

The keel-billed toucan (top), like all toucans, can seize a berry in the tip of its bill and then toss it to the back of its throat. Toco toucans (right) have the largest bills of all toucans.

Male birds of paradise, such as the emperor bird of paradise (below), attract females during the mating season by dancing and spreading their feathers.

Toucans Toucans are native to South America. Like many parrots, they nest in tree holes, live mostly in lowland tropical forests, and feed on fruit. Toucans supplement their diet with lizards, insects, and the eggs and nestlings of small birds. A thick but surprisingly lightweight bill allows them to pluck berries or seeds from branches too thin to bear their weight.

Toucans are sociable birds, preening their companions' feathers and sharing food. As part of their social behavior, two birds may engage in nonaggressive bill-wrestling. They are not faithful egg incubators—they often leave the nest unattended—but once the eggs are hatched both parents take turns feeding the nestlings. Before sleeping, toucans lay their bill on their back and fold their tail feathers over their head.

Birds of Paradise Birds of paradise are found in New Guinea, the Moluccas of Indonesia, and the tropical forests of northeastern Australia. They are rare, vividly colored non-migratory birds of the tropical forest. Adult male birds of paradise use gaudy displays of feathers and plumage to attract females, most of which have dull plumage. Because of agricultural encroachment, New Guinea's **blue bird of paradise** is especially endangered.

Vultures Vultures are among the largest scavengers of the tropical forests of South America. A solitary and endangered species, the **king vulture** is believed to have the most powerful beak of all the vultures in the Americas. Unlike most vultures, its sense of smell is weak, but its keen eyesight helps it spot carrion. Male and female king vultures are the most brilliantly colored vultures in the world.

The king vulture's bright coloring makes it stand out in its forest habitat. It does not need camouflage because it has no predators.

Eagles Three species of eagles, all of which are endangered, make their home in the crowns of emergent trees above the canopy. They are similar in appearance, having large crests, long tails, and broad, relatively short wings. The **harpy eagle** lives in the forests of Central and South America, the **crowned eagle** is found in Africa, and the **monkey-eating eagle** inhabits the Philippines. All hunt live prey such as monkeys and birds.

Nesting methods of tropical eagles are similar. They build an enormous nesting platform to accommodate the parent birds, a nestling, and any prey animals brought to the nest. The bones of prey animals remain in the nest and become part of its structure. Most eagles lay two eggs but raise only one chick. After the first egg hatches, the other is ignored. If it hatches, it is often pecked to death by the older nestling.

Huge feet, powerful talons, and massive beaks help harpy eagles catch large prey such as monkeys and sloths. Harpy eagles swoop with ease among the trees of the tropical forest.

In addition to their prominent casques, hornbills like the rhinoceros (above) and rufous hornbills (top), have special feathers above their eyes that serve as eyelashes.

Hornbills Although they resemble the toucans of the Americas, hornbills are not closely related to them. Hornbills inhabit both forests and grasslands of Africa and Asia and have long, brightly colored bills. One of the largest species is the **rhinoceros hornbill**. Most species have a *casque*, a hollow projection above the bill that acts as a resonating chamber and makes their call as loud and penetrating as a braying donkey's. The casque is larger in males and in older birds.

The beaks of many hornbills are sharp and serrated for knocking down and cutting up fruit or other food. Forest hornbills are primarily fruit eaters and are not territorial. They eat fruit and then defecate the seeds in other parts of the forest, playing an essential role in seed dispersal for forest trees.

Most hornbills nest in hollow trees. In some species, when the female is ready to lay her eggs, the male hornbill helps her block the tree hole entrance with mud, sealing the female inside. The male brings her fruit in the tip of his bill, passing it through a narrow slit left in the mud barrier. When the eggs hatch, the female feeds the chicks regurgitated fruit. The chicks come out only when they are ready to fly. This nesting method protects the hornbills from monkeys, eagles, and other predators that feed on eggs and nestlings.

The Dayak people of Borneo identify the rhinoceros hornbill as the god of war and display elaborate carvings of this bird above their longhouses.

Tropical Fish

Many tropical forests lie near river basins, such as the rain forest surrounding the basin of the Amazon River. The Amazon, the world's largest river, contains more than two thousand species of fish, an important food source for forest mammals. When water rises in the flood plains, many fish eat fruit and seeds that drop from the trees, and thus help to propagate the forest.

Piranha There are about 20 species of piranha, only four of which are considered dangerous. One species grows to be 2 feet (.6 m) long. The most familiar species, the **red piranha**, measures up to 11 inches (28 cm). It travels in schools of several hundred to several thousand and is found in lakes and rivers in northern South America, including the Amazon. Red piranha usually prey on other fish. However, they are attracted by the smell of blood and will attack a large mammal such as a tapir if it is bleeding in the water. Red piranha have extremely powerful jaws, and teeth so sharp that the Amazon Indians use them as scissors. As blood begins to flow into the water, a piranha attack becomes more and more frenzied. A school of piranha can reduce a large animal to a skeleton in a matter of minutes.

Piranha are sometimes depicted as vicious fish that readily attack humans. Reports of piranha attacks on humans are actually very rare. However, in zoos and aquariums, piranha require a separate tank to prevent them from destroying other fish.

In some regions of South America, local people consider piranha excellent fish for eating. Piranha must be caught with heavy-gauge fishing wire, because their teeth will cut through ordinary fishing lines.

Animals of the Grasslands

Every continent but Antarctica has grasslands—vast seas of grass that stretch for hundreds of square miles. Many grasslands lie in the interiors of continents, far from moderating ocean currents. Temperature changes from night to day and from season to season can be rapid and extreme. Winds blow steadily, sometimes playing delicately over the grass, sometimes whipping into violent storms. There are few trees to hide large animals, which find safety and shelter in herds.

Giraffes forage for leaves and twigs on an African grassland.

On the savanna of Tanzania in East Africa live more than 20 species of hoofed herbivores, including rhinoceroses, zebras, and elephants.

The Balance of Nature

The grasslands of the world have distinct characteristics. Tropical grasslands, known as savannas in East Africa, are usually dotted with trees and are warm all year. Savannas have long dry spells and short rainy seasons. Temperate grasslands have more distinct seasonal changes in temperature. Temperate grasslands in North America are the prairies and the Great Plains, a drier region just east of the Rocky Mountains. Other temperate grasslands include the steppes of Eurasia, the South African veld, and the South American pampas. Australia has vast dry grasslands, called outback, that merge into desert.

Because of its growth pattern, many kinds of grass can withstand heavy grazing. Grass grows from its stem base. Therefore, biting off the top of a blade of grass does not end its growth. During drought or severe cold, grass can die back to its base, remaining alive in a network of roots under the ground. The roots hold the soil in place from year to year, and animal migrations let the land rest periodically as the grass grows back. Fire can ravage a forest, but grass will grow back greener and taller, fertilized by ash. Harsh winds may fell trees, but most species of grass can bend before the wind.

Grasses

Grasses are one of the largest and hardiest families in the plant world. They can tolerate drought and blistering sunshine. There are about 10,000 different species of grass worldwide.

Grass is difficult to chew and digest, requiring a host of adaptations by grass eaters. Most grassland animals have large, flat, grinding molars for chewing grass, and special bacteria in their intestines for breaking down cellulose, a tough substance in the cell wall of plants. Some grassland animals chew the grass twice, partially digesting it the first time, in a process called *rumination* (see "Ruminants," p. 89).

Once threatened with extinction, today American bison live in protected preserves and national parks. Bison graze mostly on grass, but they also eat plants, twigs, and shrubs.

Almost all animals that live on grasslands, including meat-eaters, trace their food sources back to grass. Large predators, such as lions and leopards, hunt antelope, zebras, and other grazing animals. Scavengers such as vultures feed on the scraps left by these hunters. Hawks and other grassland birds hunt small rodents that eat the blades and seeds of grass.

Of all animal habitats, grasslands are the easiest to convert to human use. They are flat and relatively accessible, unlike mountains. They are not dense like forests or as dry as deserts. The soil is often rich and fertile. Since the beginning of recorded history, grasslands have been transformed into cultivated fields of grain and pasturelands for livestock. Today, 70 percent of the world's food supply is grown on former wild grasslands.

This conversion to farmland and pasture creates a precarious ecological balance. Cultivated fields are plowed often, leaving the soil vulnerable to erosion by wind and water. Overgrazing by pastured livestock damages the grass and wears out the land. Fences and railroads destroy animal migration paths. It has become critically important for nations around the world to learn how to protect and preserve the remaining wild grasslands for the sake of the extraordinary animals that live on them.

Grant's zebras, wilde-beests, and a Masai giraffe graze alongside one another in northern Kenya. Mixed herds are not uncommon in Africa.

African Savannas

The savannas of Africa, which cover more than one-third of that continent, include some of the world's last great tracts of grassland, home to vast numbers of buffalo, wildebeests, zebras, and other large grazing animals. Rain falls during only one or two short wet seasons of the year, followed by months of drought, when animals must migrate for food. In the rainiest regions grass may grow 10 or 12 feet high (3 to 4 m), while in drier areas it is short and sparse.

Thorn bushes, gnarled baobab trees, and flat-topped acacias dot the parched landscape of the savanna. The dryness of Africa's grasslands has been their salvation, since most of the land is unsuitable for farming and has not been settled.

Safety in Numbers

In the open African savanna, grazing animals form herds, seeking safety in numbers. If the grass is short, they are visible to roaming predators from a mile or more away, and the open landscape affords few hiding places. If the grass is tall, it may prevent animals from noticing a stalking leopard or lion. Since predators tend to single out young, old, or injured animals, some species gather around these members to protect them. One or two lookouts in a herd give warning of predators. Only one zebra need give a snort of alarm at the sight of a stalking lion, and within seconds the entire herd will gallop away.

African Buffalo African buffalo form relatively small herds of between 50 and 500. Adult males may fight each other for dominance, charging from up to 100 feet (30 m) apart and ramming their horns together. They are protected from serious harm by a horn "shield" on the crown of their heads. African buffalo usually live near the cover of trees at a forest's edge or by the reeds of a lake. They must drink at least once a day, and may drink as much as 9 gallons (34 l) of water at a time.

African buffalo are dangerous when they are attacked or frightened. Their massive horns and powerful hooves enable them to attack and kill predators such as lions.

Wildebeests Also called gnus, wildebeests are grazing antelope and form some of the most populous herds on the East African savannas. With their massive heads, slumped shoulders, and thick, curved horns, wildebeests look somewhat like domestic cattle. There are two species: the **brindled** or **blue wildebeest** and the **white-tailed wildebeest**. Wildebeests are a favored prey of big cats of the savanna, especially lions.

Wildebeests, such as the brindled gnu, graze in areas where other grazing animals or fire have kept the grass short.

At the beginning of the dry season, wildebeests form herds in the hundreds of thousands and migrate long distances to grasslands farther north. They may migrate in single file, leaving clearly marked trails across the savanna. The Serengeti region alone has about 1.5 million wildebeests. Females give birth during the winter rainy season after arriving at the northern grasslands. In the Serengeti about 400,000 calves may be born within the same three-week period.

Telling the Difference

Ears
Forehead
Tusks
Trunk
Feet

Asian elephant

African elephant

Although Asian and African elephants look similar, there are several ways to tell them apart. Of the two species, the Asian elephant is generally smaller.

- **Ears** Asian elephants have much smaller ears than African elephants.
- **Forehead** Asian elephants have a bulbous forehead; African elephants have a relatively flat forehead.
- **Tusks** Asian females and some Asian male elephants do not have any tusks at all, or have much less developed tusks than African elephants.
- **Trunks** Asian elephants have only one fingerlike projection at the tip of their trunk; African elephants have two.
- **Feet** Asian elephants usually have four nails on each hind foot; African elephants usually have three on each hind foot.

The Largest Animals of the Savanna

Elephants The largest land mammals on Earth are African bull elephants, which may stand 13 feet (4 m) tall and weigh almost 7 tons (6 mt). During the 17 hours each day that it spends eating, one elephant can eat up to 440 pounds (200 kg) of food. To obtain this enormous amount, elephants tear up grass by the roots, eat bark stripped from tree trunks, and knock down entire trees to get hard-to-reach leaves.

Elephant herds migrate over long distances to find different food sources. Herds provide elephants with communal care for their young and satisfy their need for social interaction. Most elephant herds are composed of adult females and their young. They are led by a matriarch, a dominant female who determines where the herd will travel. Adult males live separately, either in small groups or, in the case of old bulls, alone.

Elephants are highly intelligent animals. Their communications include low-frequency sounds that cannot be heard by human ears. These vocalizations enable a widely scattered herd to move at the same time and in the same direction. Migratory elephants can recall the exact topography of regions they visit from year to year, and will avoid places where something dangerous may have happened, such as an attack by poachers. When threatened, an elephant may charge, screeching, lifting its tusks, and fanning out its ears.

Elephants react to the death of a family member by clustering, sometimes for days, around the dead body or by touching the tusks and bones of the dead. About half of Africa's 1.2 million elephants were killed during the 1980s, most of them by ivory poachers. Aware that elephants were in danger of extinction, conservation groups established a worldwide ban on the ivory trade in 1989. Today, thousands of elephants live in Africa's wildlife reserves and parks.

What to look for

Elephants greet one another by touching with their trunk tips.

They flap their ears to cool off.

Asian (top) and African (below) elephant calves nurse for three to four years. They do not reach sexual maturity until they are about ten years old.

Black rhino babies travel behind their mothers for protection. Females and their young remain together until the female is ready to give birth again, in two to four years.

Rhinoceroses Rhinoceroses, or rhinos, are found on the continents of Africa and Asia. They are massive animals, weighing from 1,800 to 2,300 pounds (820–1,050 kg). Nearsighted, they rely on their keen senses of hearing and smell. To see in front of themselves, they must look out of first one eye, then the other. A rhino's olfactory passage is larger than its brain.

Rhinos lack sweat glands, and must bathe in water or roll in mud to cool off. They rest near water holes at midday, when the sun is hottest. Usually solitary animals, around water holes they tolerate the presence of other familiar rhinos.

Some rhinos are browsers, eating vegetation from trees and bushes; others are grazers, eating grass and other low ground plants. The **black rhino** of Africa is a browser, with a prehensile upper lip for grasping leaves and twigs. It can also stand on its hind legs and break off branches with its horn. The black rhino is more combative than other species of rhinos and is likely to charge the source of an unwelcome smell. It can toss a human into the air with its front horn.

The **white rhino,** which is actually light brown or gray, is a grazer. Its wide, square mouth and broad lips crop grass close to the ground. Most rhinos can eat very coarse vegetation, including acacias, which have thorns sharp enough to puncture the tire of a car.

Rhinos do not reproduce quickly or often. Their gestation period is around 16 months, and females typically have only one young every three or four years. They can live up to 45 years; thus their slow reproduction did not formerly cause a reduction in numbers. In this century, however, rhinos have been hunted relentlessly for their horns, and poaching has continued despite protective legislation. From an estimated 65,000 25 years ago, the black rhino population today has been reduced to about 2,500.

White rhino females without young often form small groups. They are easily frightened and not normally aggressive. As a defense against lions, white rhinos gather in a tight circle, facing outward.

What to look for

Adult male Indian rhinos and white rhinos are much larger than the females; in other species both males and females are about the same size.

Black and white rhinos usually have two horns, with the larger horn in front.

They rub their horns against trees and rocks.

Their legs are thick to support their massive weight.

Indian rhinoceroses have only one horn. Large folds of skin give them the appearance of wearing body armor.

Hippopotamuses African river hippopotamuses, or hippos, have a wide mouth for cropping grass close to the ground. They live in lakes and rivers and are excellent swimmers, closing their nostrils and ears before submerging. Wallowing in the water protects them from sunburn and helps to hide them from predators. The **Nile hippo** can peer through bulging eyes as if through a periscope while its body remains underwater.

The **river hippo** emerges from the water at night to graze. Like rhinos, it wears narrow paths into the ground along favorite routes between the water and grazing places. Averaging 2,500 pounds (1,130 kg), the river hippo consumes about 100 pounds (45 kg) of grass a night.

The pygmy hippo averages 500 pounds (227 kg) and has eyes on the side, not the top of its head. More land-based than the river hippo, it is an easy target for hunters and is endangered.

Hippos can open their jaws 150 degrees (top). Males often open their jaws while fighting. All hippos have smooth skin adapted to life in the water (bottom). Their skin glands secrete a fluid that protects them from sunburn and disease.

The Secrets of Camouflage

Camouflage is a method of concealment that can be used by animals for offensive or defensive purposes. It is beneficial for stalking prey or for hiding from predators. *Camouflage* originated as a military term, first used during World War I, to refer to a method of hiding weaponry, troops, or anything else from the enemy.

One kind of camouflage is background matching, or protective coloration, in which an animal resembles its background in color. For example, the coyote (shown above) of the American plains is almost the same color as the vegetation in which it is standing. Green snakes are difficult to see when they are resting in foliage. Brown snakes "disappear" against tree trunks or

Another form of camouflage is outline concealment. The collective stripes of a zebra herd make the outline of individual zebras difficult to see, and may defend the animals against blood-sucking tsetse flies which recognize potential hosts by shape. Similarly, the stripes on a tiger help to conceal its outline in tall grass.

Animals that can sting, or that taste or smell foul to predators, often have warning coloration, such as bright patterns of yellow and black, or red and black, that predators learn to avoid. The color or shape of these offensive animals is sometimes mimicked by other species. For example, the viceroy butterfly mimics the color pattern of the foul-tasting monarch butterfly. Predators are thus tricked into avoiding

A baby giraffe (left) can walk within an hour of birth. Each giraffe's coat has a unique pattern of markings. The markings provide camouflage while the animal feeds among the trees. A giraffe (bottom) uses its tongue to gather leaves into its mouth.

What to look for

Male giraffes typically have bony growths above each eye socket.

Both male and female giraffes have skin-covered horns. Adult males' horns are thicker; female horns are crowned with a tuft of black hair.

Giraffes smell, lick, and rub each other in social contact.

A bulge moving up a giraffe's throat is visible when the cud comes up for a second chewing.

Giraffes Mixed herds of giraffes, wildebeests, elephants, zebras, and other animals often graze or browse together. For a wildebeest or a zebra, traveling with giraffes makes sense, because giraffes have the keenest sight and the greatest range of vision of any large African mammal. Giraffes are also the tallest land animals, often reaching 17 feet (5 m) in height.

A giraffe's tongue is flexible and can be as long as 18 inches (46 cm). The animal's great height allows it to browse on branches that most hoofed animals cannot reach. Giraffes browse on about 60 plant species, mostly trees, shrubs, and, occasionally, vines. Because they obtain moisture from their food, giraffes can survive for weeks or months without drinking.

Giraffes can run up to 35 miles per hour (56 km/h), leap fences 6 feet (2 m) tall, and kick fiercely if provoked. Their tough hides offer protection against lions and other predators. They are vulnerable when drinking, however, since they must splay their legs awkwardly to dip their long neck down to the water. Giraffes are also vulnerable on marshy grasslands, where their relatively small feet may sink into the ground.

Odd-Toed Grassland Animals

Zebras It is no accident that a zebra looks like a horse with stripes. Both animals are part of the *equine* family and share many characteristics. All equines, for example, have an elongated head, slender legs, and hoofed feet. Of the three species of zebras, the **plains zebra** is the most common, found in eastern and southern Africa. The **mountain zebra**, native to the mountainous regions of southwest Africa, and **Grevy's zebra**, found in the dry grasslands of Ethiopia and Somalia, are both rare.

Zebra herds travel slowly so that the young are not separated from the herd and left vulnerable to predators.

Zebras can endure severe drought, living on dry grass at times when cattle are dying of starvation. Their teeth, like the teeth of horses, grow throughout their lives, an adaptation that allows them to chew tough, abrasive grasses. As they graze, zebras make so much noise cropping and chewing that predators find them easily even at night.

Sociable animals, zebras travel in family groups, which usually consist of a dominant stallion and several mares, their offspring, and occasional bachelors. At times, families combine in herds of up to five thousand. The pattern of each individual zebra's stripes is unique. Zebras probably recognize one another by smell but might also use stripe patterns for recognition. When not grazing, zebras often gently groom one another. Two zebras will stand together facing in opposite directions, each with its head on the other's back, a position that allows them both to rest and to watch for predators.

Each species of plains animal has its own flight distance from intruders that determines when it will sound an alert and run. For zebras this distance is about 100 feet (30 m). When a zebra herd flees from a predator, the dominant stallion protects the rear by kicking at whatever animal is in pursuit.

Even-Toed Grassland Animals

Zebras and horses have flat hooves, which work well on hard, rough ground. The cushioning of hooves and joints allows them to run fast and absorb the shock of ground contact. On wet or uneven ground, however, an even-toed hoof—a hoof divided into two parts—works better than a single hoof. Even-toed hooves allow animals to run quickly and still keep their footing on slippery or uneven terrain (see "Hooves," p. 180–181).

Antelope For antelope, even-toed hooves make possible a range of habitats, including mountains, wetlands, and deserts, although they are most typically grassland animals. Antelope are both agile runners and leapers. When alarmed, **impala** and **springbok antelope** may make a series of upward leaps, reaching heights of 10 to 12 feet (3 to 4 m) and bouncing over the backs of their companions. This energetic leaping releases a warning scent from a gland in their legs before they dash away.

A few species of antelope rely on their horns to protect themselves against predators. For example, a lion may be intimidated by a male **waterbuck antelope's** curved, spiraling horns, which may measure 3 feet (1 m) from base to tip. Most antelope, however, use their horns only for territorial combat with others of their own species. Both the male and female **eland antelope** have heavy spiral horns.

Two male common elands tangle horns in the final step in a confrontation ritual. The ritual begins with each covering its horns with sap and mud.

Big Cats

Leopards One of the most widespread members of the cat family, the leopard of Africa and Southern Asia has adapted to a variety of habitats, from tropical forests to dry savannas. (The so-called **"black panther"** is actually a leopard with a black coat through which traces of spots can be discerned.) Though their numbers are declining, leopards are still relatively common in parts of Africa and southern Asia, with the exception of the rare **clouded leopard** (see p. 50). They have been known to live as long as 23 years.

Solitary, nocturnal hunters, leopards have territories ranging up to 40 square miles (104 sq km). They fiercely defend their territory from competitors of the same species, and sometimes from other species. Like lions and cheetahs, they stalk their quarry, getting as close as possible before charging. They can run for short distances at a maximum speed of about 35 miles per hour (56 km/h). On the savannas their preferred diet is hoofed animals such as gazelles, but they will settle for rodents and birds if necessary.

Leopards are expert tree climbers. They sleep in trees and drag their prey there to avoid hyenas and other scavengers. Leopards have also been known to leap onto prey from tree branches.

Adapted for Speed—The Cheetah

Flexible spine is necessary for high-speed sprinting.

Long tail provides balance.

Broad nasal passage supplies oxygen to lungs and heart.

Small teeth have shallow roots to make room for wide nasal passage.

Long legs are essential for running.

Nonretractable claws provide traction.

Enlarged lungs, heart, and arteries supply oxygen for running muscles.

Cheetah Found in many parts of Africa, the cheetah, a single species, is usually a solitary hunter and weighs about 120 pounds (55 kg). Built for speed, the cheetah has long, delicate legs, raised hindquarters, and nonretractable claws that dig into dry ground like the spikes on an athlete's shoe.

The cheetah's incredible speed would seem to guarantee its success as a species, but in fact it is endangered in the wild. Unlike leopards, cheetahs are specialist hunters, which means they rely heavily on a single species of prey (usually gazelles or impalas). They cannot adapt well if that prey becomes scarce. Also, cheetahs by nature do not defend their territory and will sometimes give up their kill to lions, hyenas, or vultures.

Scientists believe that cheetahs probably came close to extinction thousands of years ago. As their numbers declined, they began inbreeding. Today all cheetahs are so closely related that they are almost identical genetically. They are slow to reproduce and vulnerable to disease. About 75 percent of cheetah cubs die within six months. These weaknesses are characteristic of inbred animals.

Male cheetahs tend to live in small groups, sometimes for life. Group members are often from the same litter. Female cheetahs are solitary animals. They avoid contact with other cheetahs until they are ready to mate.

Lion Most big cats are solitary, but the lion of the grasslands and deserts of Africa is an exception. A lion group, or pride, usually contains two adult males, several females, and cubs. Each pride of 5 to 37 lions has a fixed territory. Territorial authority is affirmed by roaring for about an hour after sundown. Intruding lions are aggressively turned away. Members of the pride mark their territory with urine and with odor from scent glands on their feet. If prey is scarce, a territory may extend for 100 square miles (260 sq km).

What to look for

Male lions are the only cats with manes.

Female lions are much smaller than male lions.

Lion cubs have spotted coats.

To cool off, lions sometimes lie on their backs.

Lions prefer to hunt in the coolest hours of the night, concealed by darkness. A hunting expedition may cover 15 square miles (40 sq km) on a moonless night. Most hunting is done by females while the males guard the hunting territory. By hunting in groups, lions can fan out and close in on a single prey from all sides. Hoofed animals, such as zebras and gazelles, are favorite prey, but lions will also kill young hippos, elephants, and even cape buffalo. Fallen prey is usually divided among the pride. A single lion can swallow 75 pounds (34 kg) of meat at one kill. Unable to compete for their share of meat, cubs sometimes starve to death during their first year.

Lions greet each other by rubbing their heads and foreheads together and releasing odors from scent glands. Females reinforce social bonds in the pride by grooming other lions. Like domestic cats, lions rake their claws vertically on trees to shed uncomfortable claw casings.

Lions have small projections on their tongues (below) to hold meat while they are feeding. At three years of age (bottom), male lions develop light-colored manes. Manes darken with age.

How Fast Do They Go?

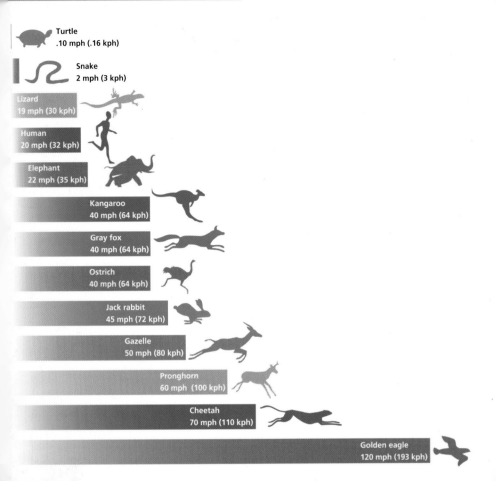

Turtle
.10 mph (.16 kph)

Snake
2 mph (3 kph)

Lizard
19 mph (30 kph)

Human
20 mph (32 kph)

Elephant
22 mph (35 kph)

Kangaroo
40 mph (64 kph)

Gray fox
40 mph (64 kph)

Ostrich
40 mph (64 kph)

Jack rabbit
45 mph (72 kph)

Gazelle
50 mph (80 kph)

Pronghorn
60 mph (100 kph)

Cheetah
70 mph (110 kph)

Golden eagle
120 mph (193 kph)

It is difficult to measure the comparative speeds of animals in the wild. Some animals are adapted for high speeds for hunting and defense purposes, but their maximum speed may differ widely from their normal pace.

The cheetah, for example, the fastest and animal over short distances, can maintain a maximum speed of 70 miles per hour (110 km/h) for distances up to a quarter of a mile (300 m). However, to catch its breath after killing its prey, a cheetah may have to pant for up to 30 minutes before starting to feed. During that time other predators, such as hyenas or lions, sometimes make off with the fresh kill.

The fastest bird, the peregrine falcon, is estimated to catch its prey at top speeds of 200 miles per hour (320 km/h). At this diving speed, it surprises a victim by striking it in the air with its feet, catching the injured bird as it falls, and carrying it away.

Male ostriches (top) form a U-shape with their necks to show submission to dominant males. The ostrich's long neck (bottom), allows the bird to peck for food on the ground. Ostriches can see great distances when their neck is raised.

Ostriches

Ostriches are the largest living birds. Four subspecies inhabit different regions of Africa. The males measure up to eight feet (2.5 m) tall and weigh up to 340 pounds (155 kg). Because of their great size, ostriches cannot fly. Instead, they run. With up to 15-foot (4.5 m) strides, they can cover the ground at speeds of 40 miles per hour (64 km/h). Two large toes on each foot provide traction equivalent to an antelope's divided hoof.

Because of their size and speed, adult ostriches have few natural enemies. Lions are reluctant to attack them because ostriches can kick with immense force. They are aggressive and have been known to charge at railroad cars. Male ostriches have a loud, booming call, used to defend their territory.

Male ostriches gather a harem of three to five females, all of whom lay their 6-inch-long (15 cm), almost spherical eggs in the same large ground nest. A typical set, or clutch, of eggs may include 15 to 50 eggs, though some clutches are larger. Only one of the hens remains with the nest. The cock and hen take turns guarding the nest and incubating the eggs. After hatching, a single cock or hen may lead as many as one hundred chicks behind it as it searches for food and water.

Because ostriches can go several days without drinking, they can live in semideserts as well as grasslands. Their soft plumage insulates them against the heat of the sun. They eat plants, seeds, and berries, and often feed among herds of antelope and zebras. Ostriches have excellent eyesight and may be the first to warn a mixed herd of an approaching predator.

Animals of the Wetlands

Flamingo and baby

Snowy egret

Pelican

Red-crowned crane

Wetlands, also called swamps or marshes, are home to many popular zoo animals. Once widely regarded as little more than breeding grounds for mosquitoes, wetlands are now acknowledged as valuable ecosystems.

Besides containing a wide variety of plant and animal life, wetlands often act as buffer zones between land and water. They absorb excess rainwater, thus minimizing the effects of flooding. Freshwater wetlands often filter pollutants from the waters flowing through them.

Today, fragile wetlands are being destroyed at an alarming rate. Developed countries drain wetlands to make way for business and residential growth in urban areas. Less developed countries "claim" wetlands for agriculture or grazing. This devastation has brought many wetland species close to extinction.

Wetland birds, many of which are endangered, feed on plants, abundant insects, frogs, and lizards. These birds include flamingos, herons, ibis, spoonbills, cranes, and storks.

Flamingos are found near lakes and coastal waters in South America, and in parts of Africa and South Asia. They fly long distances in large flocks in search of suitable feeding sites. Characterized by their long, slender legs, pink plumage, and

Roseate spoonbill

American white ibis

Alligator

Cattle egret

Goliath heron

down-turned bills, flamingos subsist on a diet of small saltwater animals and plants.

The huge Goliath heron, of Africa and Asia, stands 5 feet (1.3 m) tall and lives on fish in swampy areas. The largest American heron, the great blue heron, standing about 4 feet (1 m) tall, may add snails and small mammals to its diet. Another wetland wader, the snowy egret, is now protected in the United States. Male and female snowy egrets have beautiful 18-inch (46 cm) mating plumage.

Pelicans are found near coastal regions and lakes in parts of Asia and the Americas. They have short, strong legs adapted for swimming and a pouch under

their bill for scooping up fish.

Crocodiles and alligators live in tropical and subtropical wetlands around the world. The American alligator, found in the southeastern United States, basks on marshy river banks and preys on birds, fish, mammals, and turtles. Any animal that dares enter or even approach its waters is fair game.

One mammal found in south-Asian wetlands, the fishing cat, preys on fish, birds, and insects. The fishing cat has been decimated by hunters for its light-brown spotted coat. Other mammals, such as elephants and zebras, may migrate to wetlands when grasslands are dry.

A hyena's famous laugh may be a sign of distress at being attacked or chased or may mean the discovery of a good food source. Hyenas sometimes whoop and howl spontaneously when they are alone.

Unlike other hyenas, spotted hyenas hunt and kill most of their own food. A single spotted hyena can chase and bring down an adult wildebeest. Spotted hyenas hide leftover food for later consumption.

Life in the Pack

Hyenas The three species of hyenas are often mistaken for dogs but are most closely related to mongooses and civets. Scavengers, they feast on the kill of lions and other big cats. They also are predators in their own right, hunting at night in packs of up to 40 animals. Hyenas have excellent night vision and prey upon hoofed animals that do not see as well in the dark. With their powerful jaws, hyenas can crush even the largest bones of cattle, and they digest not only flesh but bones and hide.

The most common species of hyena is the **spotted hyena**, native to most of the African savannas. Spotted hyenas have a coarse, woolly coat, with black spots on a dull yellow background. Females are larger than males and dominate hyena society. Spotted hyenas form clans of up to 80 members, depending on the species. Each clan has a central underground den in which all of the clan females bear their cubs.

Hunting Dog A single species, the African hunting dog, or wild dog, resembles the hyena—its powerful jaw muscles give it the same massive head. Hunting dogs run in packs of about 10 animals, sometimes as many as 60. Each pack has its own territory, but because hunting dogs are nomadic, the territory is not permanent. The pack commonly hunts gazelles, but a large pack may attack a zebra or a young wildebeest. African hunting dogs are tireless runners, maintaining speeds of 25 miles per hour (40 km/h) over long distances.

In a pack, African hunting dogs move their large, round ears to signal to one another.

Pups are suckled for about three weeks in a communal den; older pups are fed with meat regurgitated by the adults. Hunting dogs share their kills peacefully and allow pups old enough to run with the pack to feed first. Communal life is essential to African hunting dogs. Individual dogs cannot catch prey on their own and will eventually die if separated from the pack.

North American Grasslands

Coyote In size halfway between a wolf and a fox, the coyote, a single species, is one of the most successful predators of the plains. Coyotes prey on small mammals, such as rabbits and rodents, as well as on fish, birds, deer, and carrion. They usually hunt alone or in pairs but occasionally form packs to bring down a hoofed animal such as a pronghorn. They can run almost 40 miles per hour (64 km/h). Active primarily at dusk and at night, they often howl after dark. Their quavering and mournful cries announce their location to other coyotes or establish their right to a territory.

Coyotes are among the few plains animals to have flourished in the wake of human settlement. Since the late nineteenth century they have steadily extended their range, and are now found throughout the United States and southern Canada. Coyotes are opportunists. Like foxes, they manage to live and thrive near human settlements. They often follow tractors or herds of cattle to catch rodents startled out of the grass.

Coyotes have benefited from the disappearance of rival predators, such as wolves and bobcats, and from the cutting down of forests. Their large litters and varied diet have also helped them flourish. Whereas loss of habitat has threatened the survival of bison, black-footed ferrets (see p. 93), and other grasslands animals, for coyotes it has represented a chance to outcompete less adaptable animals.

Coyotes survive harsh winters by eating the remains of dead animals, such as deer and cattle. Young coyotes are born in the spring and nurse for seven weeks. By late summer they are strong enough to hunt and survive on their own.

Bison Before the first European traders arrived in the 1600s, an estimated 50 to 75 million migratory bison, also called *buffalo*, grazed on the Great Plains, the vast grasslands that stretched between the Mississippi River and the Rocky Mountains. They were also common in hardwood forests east of the Mississippi. American Indians hunted bison and used every part of the animal: the flesh for food, the horns for cups, the bones for tools, and the hide for clothing and tents.

Beginning in the mid-1800s, settlement of the Great Plains decimated the bison population. Farms and railroads disrupted bison migrations, and hunters shot them by the millions. By 1900 there were fewer than 1,000 wild bison left in all of North America. With government help, naturalists rescued the survivors. By the early 1990s about 50,000 bison were living on stretches of prairie conserved as national parks.

Bison are massive creatures, standing more than 6 feet (2 m) tall and weighing up to 2,200 pounds (1,000 kg). Because of their thick coat, they are well adapted to harsh prairie weather. The shaggy head is the most heavily insulated part of their body, and during blizzards bison stand facing into the wind. Bison find

American bison were first called *buffalo* by Europeans in 1635 because they resembled the buffalo of Africa and Asia. However, African and Asian buffalo are the only true buffalo.

Bison Tracking

Frontier settlers of the eighteenth century crossed the Appalachian Mountains on old "buffalo roads," created by migrating buffalo—like the path that led through the Cumberland Gap. One buffalo road that led into northern Ohio eventually became the route of the New York Central railroad.

Ruminants

Impala antelope

Ruminants are even-toed grazing animals that digest the tough grass they eat by "chewing their cud." Ruminants include bison, buffalo, antelope, cattle, sheep, and goats.

Most ruminants have a four-chambered stomach. They swallow their food rapidly; then it passes to the first chamber of the stomach, where digestion starts. Later, when the animals are resting, they regurgitate the food and chew it again. The rechewed food is swallowed, and further digestion occurs in the third and fourth compartments of the stomach. Digestion continues in the small intestine.

Because ruminants gulp down food and chew it later, they can stay alert for predators. More importantly, they can use hard-to-digest grasses and leaves as food.

grass in winter by sweeping their head from side to side to brush the snow away from the ground. In spring they roll on the ground to rub off the remains of their heavy winter coat. Their habit is first to graze in the morning, rest and *ruminate*, or chew their cud, at midday, and graze again in the evening.

During the winter, male and female bison gather in separate herds. Some herds migrate to warmer areas to find food. Male and female herds come together to mate during the summer.

Horns

Blackbuck

Scimitar-horned oryx

Horns are hard, pointed growths that appear on the heads of many mammals, both male and female. Antelope, cattle, pronghorn, and sheep are all horned animals.

Like antlers, horns grow from bones in the skull. Horns grow continuously and, unlike antlers, are not shed each year. One exception to this are the horns of the pronghorn. The outer sheath of its black

Pronghorn Pronghorn, a single species, are found only in North America and belong to a family of their own, distinct from antelope. Like bison, pronghorn are ruminants, and their teeth are adapted for browsing on coarse grasses and shrubs. Their prominent eyes give them 360-degree vision if they turn their heads. Pronghorn form large, mixed herds in fall and winter but separate, by sex, into smaller herds during spring and summer.

Pronghorn are the fastest land animals in the Americas, able to run up to 60 miles per hour (100 km/h). By the time it is four days old, a pronghorn fawn can outrun a human. When pronghorn are alarmed, their muscles contract and a patch of white fur on their haunches stands up, flashing a warning that can be seen by other pronghorns 2 miles (3 km) away. They also release a musky scent that warns of danger.

Pronghorn numbered about 40 million when the first European settlers arrived. By 1915 there were fewer than 15,000 left. Today, conservation programs have increased their numbers to more than half a million.

horns is shed annually.

Horns have a bony core covered by a layer of keratin, a tough, waterproof substance rich in protein. Keratin is also a substance found in hair and fingernails.

Males use their horns to establish dominance during the mating season. Often a display of horns is enough to avoid fights. Horns are also used to protect animals against predators.

What to look for

Female antelope have shorter horns than males, and sometimes their horns are hardly visible.

Male antelope use their scent glands, located on their ears, rump, and toes, to mark territory.

Pronghorn bucks have black, hooked horns. They also have black facial markings, including two patches beneath the ears. The markings play a significant role in mating rituals and displays of male dominance.

Digging in on the Prairie

Prairie Dog Although it barks like a dog when excited or alarmed, the prairie dog is actually a species of ground squirrel. It feeds on insects such as grasshoppers, and on grasses near its burrows. Unlike most squirrels, it breeds only once a year. Both sexes care for the young.

For mutual defense on the open prairie, prairie dogs dig burrows close together, forming "towns" composed of chambers that are connected by long tunnels. Prairie dog towns are hard to miss: throughout the town prairie dogs cut down every plant more than 6 inches (15 cm) high. This allows them to see in all directions, especially when they are sitting upright on the mound of earth at the opening of their burrow. Sociable, related clans of prairie dogs share the same neighborhood, scurrying from burrow to burrow and rubbing noses to identify or greet one another. An unknown prairie dog from another part of town will likely be chased away. If a predator is spotted, one alarm call will prompt an entire town to dash to its burrows.

Burrowing rodents such as prairie dogs are an important part of the grasslands ecosystem. By digging underground tunnels, they carry fresh soil to the surface and bring air to the packed earth, like a gardener turning over the soil with a spade. The conversion of the prairies to farmland and the poisoning of prairie dogs by ranchers has greatly reduced the prairie dog population in the wild. This, in turn, has reduced the numbers of other animals adapted to live in and around prairie dog towns.

Prairie dog burrows usually have two openings that provide air circulation and an escape route from predators. Soil mounds at the entrance help prevent flooding of the burrow.

Prairie dogs feed on plants that grow outside their burrows. At the National Zoo, this natural behavior is encouraged by placing the animals' food near the burrows.

Black-Footed Ferret The black-footed ferret once lived near prairie dog towns and specialized in preying on prairie dogs. This slender ferret, native to western North America, has pale fur streaked with brown, a black mask over its eyes and—true to its name—black feet. A solitary animal, it usually hunts at night. By the 1970s it was believed to be extinct.

In the early 1980s, however, a small population of black-footed ferrets was discovered in Wyoming. When disease caused this group to dwindle, the U.S. Fish and Wildlife Service decided to capture the last 18 survivors for zoo breeding. Now the National Zoo in Washington, D.C. participates in a breeding program that has already returned some zoo-bred ferrets to undisturbed prairie dog towns in Wyoming.

Black-footed ferrets not only eat prairie dogs but also use their burrows for shelter. Intensive zoo breeding has increased the black-footed ferret population to 450 animals.

Birds of Prey of the Prairies

Hawks and eagles hunt over grasslands for prey such as mice, rabbits, squirrels, and prairie dogs. Prairie dogs have a specific alarm call just for hawks and eagles, and it is their most urgent warning against an approaching enemy. Though birds of prey cannot pursue prairie dogs into their burrows, they can drop with sudden and dangerous accuracy out of the sky.

Hawks and Eagles Some birds of prey, such as the **golden eagle** and the **red-tailed hawk**, nest at the edge of grasslands, usually in a treetop or on a rocky crag high above the plain. Others, such as the **northern harrier**, a hawk of North America and Eurasia, nest on the ground in dense undergrowth. Northern harriers nest on marshes and sand dunes as well as grasslands.

The materials that hawks use for their nests depend on the nest's location. Near farmlands, red-tailed hawks line their nests with cornstalks. Hawks on the Great Plains build nests of cow or horse dung, sagebrush roots, and bleached animal bones.

Red-tailed hawks lay one to four eggs in the spring and sit on them until they hatch a month later. At six weeks, the young hawks are mature enough to learn to fly. The parents continue to share the nest even after the fledglings are gone, and most pairs mate for life.

Hawks and eagles are expert soarers, able to float upward or downward on air currents. Golden eagles, which nest in mountains but sometimes hunt over grasslands, can soar for hours on partly folded wings. From a distance they appear to be circling lazily in the sky, but in fact they are moving with great speed. Golden eagles can glide at speeds of about 120 miles per hour (190 km/h), and make vertical dives at 150 to 200 miles per hour (240 to 320 km/h).

The wingspan of eagles, such as the golden eagle (top), can reach up to 7 feet (2 m). Hawks, such as the ferruginous hawk (bottom), have excellent eyesight for spotting prey and thick talons for catching it.

Australian Grasslands

Kangaroos In spite of agricultural encroachment, millions of kangaroos live in the grasslands bordering the vast Australian desert. Kangaroos are marsupials, animals that raise their young in an abdominal pouch (see "Marsupials" on pp. 150–151). Protected for 5 to 11 months in their mother's pouch, baby kangaroos benefit from the mother's speed and survival skills.

The most common kangaroos, found throughout continental Australia, are the **red kangaroo,** with a body length of 65 inches (1.5 m), and the **wallaroo** or **hill kangaroo,** which grows to about 49 inches (1.25 m). Midway between these two in size is the **eastern gray kangaroo,** native to eastern Australia and Tasmania. Smaller species include the **rufous rat kangaroo.** All are herbivores.

Like antelope, kangaroos use speed as a defense. They can travel over long distances at 25 miles (40 km) per hour and can run in short bursts at 30 to 40 miles (48 to 64 km) per hour. They use their powerful hind legs and sharp claws for defense, and can rip open a predator's belly with one well-aimed blow. Their defensive and reproductive strategies have helped kangaroos compete successfully with humans for the use of grazing land.

Kangaroos, such as the red kangaroo (top) and Tasmanian gray kangaroo (bottom), use their tails for balance and support while hopping or standing. They can travel 26 feet (8 m) in one jump.

What to look for

Kangaroos' short forelegs in proportion to long hindlegs are adapted to hopping.

They have flexible toes for grooming.

To cool themselves, kangaroos lick the inside of their forearms, where blood vessels are close to the skin.

Baby Animals and Their Survival Strategies

Young Indian elephant   Ju

For most baby animals, the first weeks of life are precarious. Smaller and slower-moving than their parents, baby animals are easy targets for predators. Those grasslands animals with no den or tree to hide in are especially vulnerable.

Many hoofed grasslands animals give birth quickly. Wildebeests give birth in less than an hour, in a place no more protected than a patch of long grass. Baby giraffes enter the world by dropping several feet to the ground, an unceremonious end to a delivery that takes about 45 minutes.

Newborn grasslands animals often are well developed. Antelope calves can run an hour after birth; so can zebras. Giraffes are 6 feet tall (2 m) at birth and weigh 150 pounds (68 kg). Ostrich chicks are a foot (.3 m) tall at hatching. They can run fast and eat vegetation as soon as their feathers are dry.

Animals with dens usually give birth to less well-developed young. Coyote pups are blind and helpless at birth. Cheetah babies, born in a thicket or cave, are also blind at birth and weigh less than a pound. Although hyena pups are born with their eyes open, they spend their first six to eight weeks of life protected in an underground den.

Some baby animals imprint, or identify, the nearest, most frequently seen object as their mother, and look to it for food and security. A mother zebra and her foal keep apart from all members of their group for several days after the foal is born, during which time imprinting takes place.

A joey or baby kangaroo in its mother's pouch

Elephants engage in cooperative care of their young, an effective strategy for animals that are naturally social. Baby elephants may be nursed by any nursing female in the herd, not just by the mother. In large elephant herds, a young female sometimes takes care of several elephant calves. Nursing lions and hyenas will also suckle cubs that are not their own.

Prairie dogs, also sociable animals, protect their pups in an elaborate system of underground burrows. During their first summer, pups are cared for by both males and females. Kangaroo babies, called *joeys,* spend the first five to eleven months of life protected in their mother's pouch.

Because large predators tend to stalk herds, some animals separate their young from the herd. African antelope sometimes leave their calves alone in the grass while they graze at a distance. Mother eland graze apart from their calves, coming back at intervals during the day to nurse them. However, American bison protect their young by keeping them near the center of the herd.

Female cats such as cheetahs and leopards must leave their litter only a few days after birth in order to hunt for food. (Female lions share in the kills of the pride, and therefore usually stay with their cubs.) Female leopards sometimes leave their litter for up to two days. To disguise the den's location (and to keep the den clean), the female consumes her cubs' excrement and buries her own feces. Female leopards may change the location of their den several times.

Animals of the Desert

Deserts are hostile places for most living things. Water is scarce or absent, and temperatures fluctuate wildly. Some deserts are blazing hot; others are cold and bleak. In some, dry winds blow across dunes of drifting sand in which it is impossible for animals to dig a burrow. Yet a surprising number of mammals, birds, amphibians, insects, reptiles, and plants have evolved intricate survival strategies for this forbidding habitat.

As a pack animal, the Arabian camel can carry up to 500 pounds (230 kg) for long distances in desert heat.

The Challenge of the Desert

Most deserts receive no more than 10 inches (25 cm) of precipitation a year, and some have no rain for years at a time. Yet desert animals must have water to stay alive. Some animals stay near springs and water holes or migrate to borderlands where rainfall is greater. Others survive on moisture from their prey. Where available, desert animals use the water in grass and plants, but in the hottest deserts, such as the Sahara, plants are exceedingly rare.

Most desert animals have evolved ways to conserve water. Some animals, for example, exhale or excrete minimal amounts of moisture. Fresh camel dung is so low in moisture that it can be burned as fuel almost immediately, unlike most animal dung which must dry before it can be burned.

Desert plants sometimes serve as emergency supplies of water for desert animals. Cacti, such as the giant saguaro, absorb water quickly during infrequent rains and store it in thick, pulpy stems, where it is available to animals such as desert woodrats, jackrabbits, pronghorn, and peccaries. Some animals lick the dew that settles on vegetation overnight. Others eat the seeds and fruits of moisture-retaining plants. To deter animals from eating them, some succulent plants, such as the little leaf horsebrush shrub, have evolved toxic spines.

Cactus plants, such as the plains prickly pear (below), have sharp protective spines. Prickly pears grow in parts of North America and Hawaii.

Too Hot and Too Cold

Extremes of heat and cold are the desert's second major challenge for its inhabitants. Air temperatures ranging up to 130°F (54°C) have been measured in deserts such as Death Valley in the United States, and the African Sahara. Rock and sand absorb heat just as an asphalt pavement does, making the ground surface hotter than the air. At night, the temperature can drop below freezing in some desert regions.

Some animals escape the daytime desert heat by burrowing underground or by lying in the shade of rocks or plants. Other animals live in the branches of large cacti. Desert squirrels, such as antelope squirrels, may sit in the shadow cast by their own tails. Reptiles depend on the sun for warmth but seek shade when they become hot. Many desert mammals have fur that insulates them from extreme temperatures. Their coats may be pale gray or yellow, to reflect heat and act as camouflage. Very few animals can endure the blazing noontime sun.

Nighttime brings another extreme. The same clear skies that allow the sun's rays to warm the ground during the day also let stored heat escape after the sun sets. The temperature falls steadily all night, often reaching the freezing point before dawn. Burrowing animals seek shelter during the coldest hours of the night, just as they do during the heat of noon. Cold-blooded animals such as reptiles, whose body temperatures are largely determined by the temperature of their environment, retreat to the relative warmth of burrows or crevices as the night gets colder.

Desert scrub and sand provide camouflage for the western diamondback rattlesnake (left). It lives as far south as the deserts of northwest Mexico (right).

A Changing Habitat

Under the influence of wind and weather, deserts change more quickly than other habitats. Today, many of the world's deserts are growing larger. In some regions, overgrazing by livestock has damaged nearby grasslands, turning them into desert. By one estimate, the total area of desert in the world grows by 40 square miles (100 sq km) a day.

The bobcat's sand-colored coat (top left) provides camouflage from predators. Black ear tufts are a distinctive feature of the caracal (top right). The sandcat (below) has short, strong legs for digging burrows to escape the desert heat.

Desert Cats

Some animals have adapted to both temperate and desert environments. Members of the cat family found in deserts include the **caracal**, the sandcat of African savannas and Asian deserts, and its relative, the North American **bobcat**. Excellent jumpers, caracal can leap high enough to catch low-flying birds.

Bobcat The bobcat, a single species, is also known as the red **lynx** or desert wildcat. It lives in the semideserts and hills of Mexico and North America. Bobcats also live in the eastern United States, including New England. Their stumpy, bobbed tail, only about 6 inches (15 cm) long, gives them their name. Adult bobcats are about 2 feet (60 cm) tall at the shoulder. They must live where they can find steady drinking water.

Bobcats are solitary and have fixed territories. They stalk small rodents, rabbits, and birds, and occasionally hunt larger prey, such as young bighorn sheep or small deer. During the mating season, bobcats sometimes call at night, sounding like alley cats on a backyard fence.

To hide her cubs from predators, a female caracal may move them to a new location each day.

Design for the Desert

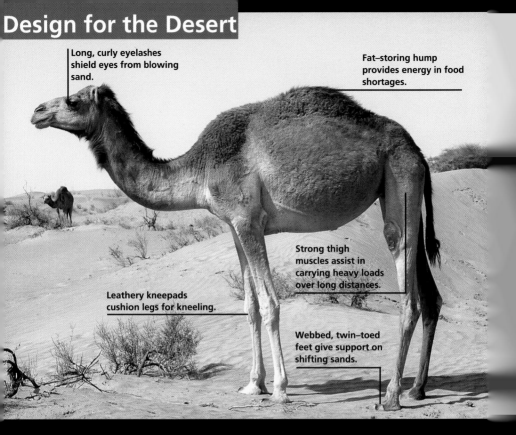

Long, curly eyelashes shield eyes from blowing sand.

Fat–storing hump provides energy in food shortages.

Strong thigh muscles assist in carrying heavy loads over long distances.

Leathery kneepads cushion legs for kneeling.

Webbed, twin–toed feet give support on shifting sands.

Camels may look comical with their splayed feet, knobby knees, and rounded chests, but they are functionally designed. Their webbed, padded toes allow them to cross the sand without sinking, and knee pads protect them when they kneel. Their ears are furred both inside and out to protect them from blowing sand.

A camel's hair is thicker on the back, where it gives protection from the sun, and thinner on the belly, for coolness. Long eyelashes and bushy eyebrows protect their eyes from sun and sand and, during sandstorms, camels are able to close their slit-like nostrils. With their leathery mouths and tongues, camels can chew on the horniest desert plants, while their sturdy

The one-humped camel of Arabia and Africa, called the dromedary, was domesticated and herded at least 5,000 ago in Mesopotamia. The original wild species has long been extinct. The two-humped, or Bactrian, camel of Asia has also been domesticated. A few small herds of wild Bactrian camels may still exist in Mongolia.

Domestic camels are invaluable as pack animals. They can travel 300 miles (483 km) in 10 days without grazing or drinking water. When they reach an oasis, they may gulp down as much as 22 gallons (85 l) of water in a single drink. Camels store fat, not water, in their hump. They burn up the fat in the hump for energy when they must go for long periods in dry regions without

Kit foxes (above and right) live in burrows that may have up to 24 openings. The foxes either dig the burrows themselves or enlarge the burrows made by small rodents.

Desert Foxes

Two members of the dog family, the American kit fox and the fennec fox of the African Sahara and Middle Eastern deserts, have adapted to desert life in strikingly similar ways. Both of these small foxes have evolved large ears that have a network of tiny blood vessels just under the skin. When air blows across the skin, it cools the blood flowing underneath. This kind of independent development of the same trait in response to similar environmental pressures is known as convergent evolution.

Kit Fox The kit fox, also known as the swift fox, lives in the American Southwest and northern Mexico and is a small, swift runner. A mature kit fox weighs 4 to 6 pounds (2–3 kg) and is rarely more than 3 feet (1 m) long, including its bushy tail. The kit fox's keen hearing is useful for hunting small rodents and lizards at night. It also preys upon birds' eggs. Kit foxes can survive for long periods on moisture from their prey.

When the female is nursing, the male hunts, bringing meat back to the underground den. A litter of five fox pups can eat nearly a pound (.5 kg) of meat every 24 hours.

Fennec Fox Typically weighing less than 3 pounds (1.5 kg), the fennec fox is the smallest member of the dog family. A nocturnal hunter, it can leap nearly 3 feet (1 m) to pounce on prey, which it pins under large paws. The fennec's ability to sense the location of a moving animal up to a mile (1.5 km) away helps it to avoid predators, such as striped hyenas, and to track small prey, including rodents, lizards, and insects. Fennecs sometimes vary their diet with fruit such as dates.

Fennecs are adapted to the desert in other ways as well. Their sandy-colored fur provides excellent camouflage, and for coolness and safety they can dig burrows up to 20 feet (6 m) in length.

Fennec foxes (above and below) can dig burrows quickly to escape from predators and to capture burrowing prey. Fennecs live in groups of 10 to 15 animals.

What to look for

Both fennec and kit foxes have long hair covering the soles of their feet, which enables them to walk on sand without sinking.

The ears of fennec foxes may measure up to 6 inches (15 cm) in length, making them much larger than the ears of kit foxes.

Communities Underground

Burrowing is one way that animals avoid desert heat. In most deserts the ground is relatively cool below the first few inches of sand or soil. Even on the hottest summer days the temperature in an underground burrow seldom rises above 68°F (20°C). Most burrowing animals, such as Australian wombats, are nocturnal. They hunt during the first half of the night, returning underground in the cool hours before dawn. One exception are meerkats, which are active during the day. Most burrowers dig individual or family burrows. A few, like wombats, build complex underground communal burrows.

Wombats Large burrowing marsupials with silky gray fur, wombats are related to koalas (see "Marsupials," pp. 150–151). The two species of adult wombats average 3 feet (1 m) in length and weigh up to 60 pounds (27 kg). They have rounded muzzles, short legs, and strong claws, which they use to dig tunnels up to 100 feet (30 m) long. Wombats look unathletic, but they move surprisingly quickly when chased and can run up to 25 miles per hour (40 km/h). The dingo, a native Australian wild dog, is the major predator of wombats.

Wombats have a slow metabolism and drink little water. Unlike other marsupials, they grow razor-sharp incisors, similar to those of rodents, in both their upper and lower jaws. Continuously growing teeth help them eat coarse grasses. Bacteria in their digestive system break down the tough fibers in their diet.

Baby wombats are born after a gestation period of less than a month. Like other young marsupials, they move directly into their mother's pouch. A wombat's pouch opens toward the birth canal, so the newborn are closer to the pouch than baby kangaroos. Young wombats leave the pouch at six or seven months, but return occasionally during the next few months to suckle.

During winter months, wombats such as the hairy-nosed wombat, bask in the sun to keep warm. Wombats do not sweat, and their waste products contain little water.

Life in a Sand Dune

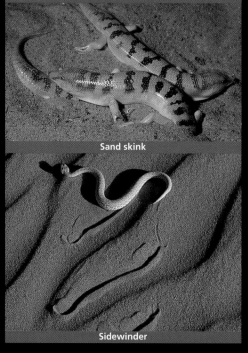

Sand skink

Sidewinder

Sand dunes present unusual challenges for the creatures that live in them. Sand dunes shift gradually under the influence of the wind, and animal burrows built in sand collapse easily. Therefore, animals found on sand dunes often dig their burrows in harder soil nearby.

Some lizards, such as the North African sand skink, or sandfish, "swim" through the sand on tiny legs. Very short legs enable sandfish to move quickly just below the surface of the sand. On other lizards, the legs have vanished altogether.

To gain traction on loose sand, small American rattlesnakes, called sidewinders, move by means of shifting loops and rolls. The horned viper of the Sahara independently evolved the same adaptation for sand dune travel.

Meerkats The Kalahari Desert and other dry lands of southern Africa are home to meerkats, which are **mongooses.** Meerkats have pointed muzzles, black ears, eye patches, black-tipped tails, and pale fur with dark stripes. They are slender animals, weighing an average of 2 pounds (1 kg).

During the day meerkats forage for insects, frogs, lizards, small rodents, and eggs by turning over stones and sniffing in crevices. They often sit on their haunches near their burrow entrances. Like prairie dogs of the North American plains, they bark a warning when predators approach.

Up to 30 meerkats live in colonies of elaborate underground burrows. They usually mate in the early fall, bearing litters of two to five young about 3 months later. They are easy to tame, and South Africans often keep them as house pets or to control mice.

Meerkats sometimes stand fully erect, balancing on the tips of their back feet. In this posture they look solemn, curious, and oddly human.

The Merriam's kangaroo rat (above) is the smallest kangaroo rat found in the United States. Kangaroo rats have excellent hearing for detecting predators. In the cold winters of some Asian deserts, the jerboa (right) hibernates for up to seven months in a burrow insulated with camel's hair or other fibers.

Strategies for Movement

Temperature extremes are not the only dangers of desert life. Open landscape offers little protection from predators. Speed helps protect desert rodents such as kangaroo rats, jerboas, gerbils, and jackrabbits, as they travel long distances to look for food and water.

Kangaroo Rats Found in the American desert, tiny kangaroo rats are only 5 or 6 inches (13–15 cm) long, but at top speed they can jump 6 feet (2 m) or farther using their hind legs.

Kangaroo rats may keep the same burrow for generations, deepening it and adding new chambers until the protective mound of sand at the entrance is several feet high. They use their short forelegs to dig their burrow, kicking away the piled-up sand with their hind legs and sealing the entrance with sand. This keeps the air inside moist, trapping humidity from the animals' breath and from stored seeds.

Jerboas Twenty-nine species of jerboas are found in habitats ranging from the hot African Sahara to the colder, steppe deserts of China and Mongolia. Jerboas travel up to 9 miles (14 km) a night searching for insects, seeds, and roots. Like kangaroo rats, they obtain moisture from their food and do not need drinking water. If food is unavailable in the hottest summer months, jerboas may *estivate*, lying dormant in a state similar to hibernation.

Gerbils In common with other desert rodents, gerbils have proportionately longer hind legs for running and jumping. They are found in African and Asian deserts. In the cold desert plateaus of central Asia and Mongolia, one species of gerbil, the **jird**, has developed a communal lifestyle, sharing food stores and a common burrow with other jirds during the harsh winter.

What to look for

Jerboas have tiny front legs, and long hind legs that enable them to jump as far as 9 feet (3 m).

Jerboas can also leap upward to snatch leaves from bushes.

By shifting their tails, they can change direction abruptly even when jumping at top speed.

The Saguaro Cactus

Saguaro cactus with spring blossoms

Gila woodpecker and nest in a saguaro cactus

Though deserts have no trees for birds and small animals to nest in, they offer other safe dwelling places. In the American Southwest, the giant, long-armed saguaro cactus provides shelter and nourishment for desert creatures. Bats, moths, and insects feed on the nectar of the saguaro's white flowers. Animals such as squirrels and mice eat its juicy, red fruit. A variety of desert creatures make their home in the saguaro's trunk that grows up to 50 feet (15 m) tall.

Like an underground burrow, a saguaro cactus hole is cooler in the daytime and warmer at night than the air outside, and its humidity is higher than that of the dry desert air. Its height above the desert floor keeps its occupants safe from predators.

The Gila woodpecker nests in the saguaro, pecking out a hole in the juicy flesh of the cactus trunk. Woody scar tissue

forms around the opening of the hole, making the nest permanent and protecting the cactus from water loss.

Gila woodpeckers use their cactus nest for only one year, digging out a new nest in a different saguaro each spring. Often the old holes are taken over by other birds, including elf owls, sparrow hawks, and cactus wrens. Sometimes brown bats, bees, and even pack rats and cactus mice move into an empty woodpecker hole. The rats and mice gnaw a spiral tunnel from the ground to the nest, feeding on the pulp of the saguaro as they go.

The ribs and grooves that run lengthwise down a saguaro cactus can expand and contract, enabling the saguaro to store water. The cactus can continue to produce flowers and fruit during times of drought because of this ability to conserve moisture.

Jackrabbits, such as the black-tailed jackrabbit (left), shed and grow new coats in response to changes in seasonal temperatures. The antelope jackrabbit (below) obtains moisture from cacti and yucca plants.

Jackrabbits Champion runners and jumpers, the jackrabbits of the North American desert are actually hares, which are larger and faster than rabbits. Their efficient metabolism requires little water and they can survive on the meager moisture contained in the driest plants.

Jackrabbits do not excavate burrows. In summer they stay cool by crouching in a shallow depression dug in grass or scrubby bushes or they may creep into a burrow dug by a tortoise or another animal.

When they feed at night, they must be on the alert for coyotes, bobcats, hawks, and owls. Their sharp sense of hearing warns them of predators, and their muscular hind legs give them speed to increase their chance of escape.

Jackrabbits, in common with other hares, sometimes communicate by thumping their hind feet on the ground. Male jackrabbits fight during the mating season, boxing with their forefeet and kicking each other with powerful hind legs. Jackrabbit populations grow quickly, with three or four litters a year of up to six young each. Like all hares, jackrabbits are born with their eyes open and a full coat of hair, and can walk soon thereafter.

What to look for

Jackrabbits, like foxes, have large ears to keep them cool.

During the day jackrabbits hold their ears erect for maximum cooling.

On cold nights they flatten their ears against their bodies.

Migrating in Search of Food and Water

Although many small desert mammals can survive without a regular water supply, most larger animals cannot. In grasslands, mammals migrate along fixed routes with the coming of the dry season. In the desert, however, the dry season predominates, and it is hard to predict when and where rain will fall. Vegetation soon withers once rainfall ceases, and animals must journey to find still-edible leaves or plants or temporary pools of rainwater.

Desert Antelope

Several species of antelope have adapted to life in dry regions. The addax of the African Sahara and oryxes of the Middle Eastern deserts and parts of North and West Africa may travel up to 50 miles (80 km) a day in search of food, looking for places where rain has fallen recently enough to produce fresh plant growth.

Fringe-eared oryx drink from pools of water. When water cannot be found, oryx dig for moisture-rich roots and bulbs.

Nocturnal Animals in Zoos

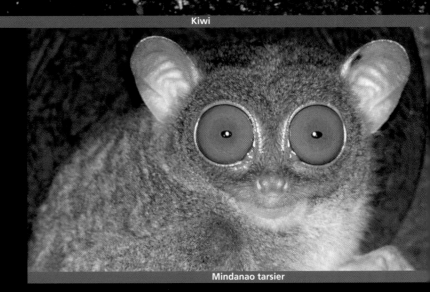

Kiwi

Mindanao tarsier

Nocturnal animals rest during the day and become active at night. Bats fly in search of fruit, nectar, or insects. Desert animals emerge from their burrows. New Zealand's kiwi birds sniff the ground with their nostril-tipped beaks in search of worms. Coyotes stalk and howl. Raccoons hunt for rodents. Alligators and crocodiles wallow in grassy swamps and prey on rabbits, minks, armadillos, and rats.

Nocturnal animals have a number of adaptations to facilitate their nightly activities. Bats, for example, find their way around by echolocation, using their ears to pick up the echoes of their high-pitched squeaks.

Mouse lemurs, bushbabies, aye-ayes, and lorises have huge eyes enabling them to see in dim light. Members of the cat and dog families, such as leopards and foxes, have a

Clouded leopard

Sugar-glider

special reflective layer in their retina that increases their night vision.

Zoos make it possible for visitors to see some nighttime activity by creating darkness for nocturnal animals during the day. At the Bronx Zoo, day and night are reversed in a stunning display called World of Darkness. In the darkened interior of a large building, infrared lights allow people to see the animals, but the animals, unaffected by the light, behave as if it were dark.

More than 200 bats, from six species, fly about in small caves. An underground tunnel houses huge Indian-crested porcupines and their young. Sugar-gliders, sloths, skunks, and bushbabies go about their business while ring-tailed cats groom themselves as they would in the desert. When the zoo closes for the night, the lights are turned on and the animals sleep as if it were day.

What to look for

Addaxes have round tufts of dense black hair in the middle of their foreheads.

Their long tails are also tipped with tufts of black hair.

Addaxes in zoos need space to roam. At the San Diego Wild Animal Park (below) and the Fossil Rim Wildlife Center in Glen Rose, Texas, addaxes live in herds of nearly one hundred animals.

Addax The addax are medium-sized antelope with long spiral horns (see "Horns," pp. 90–91; and "Antelope," p. 78). Addaxes live in small herds in dry parts of the African Sahara. They can tolerate great heat, although they seek shade from the noon sun. Broad, splayed hooves let them walk on sand without sinking. Their excellent sense of smell can locate fresh grass and leaves, which, together with small amounts of dew, provide all the water they need. Even in a zoo, they do not drink water.

Once common in North Africa and the Middle East, addaxes are now nearly extinct. Like rhinoceroses and tigers, they have been hunted as trophies and for use in folk medicine. The few hundred addaxes left in the wild now live in Niger, West Africa.

Oryx There are three species of oryxes—fast, sturdy antelope, strikingly patterned in brown, black, and white. Their horns are 3 to 5 feet long (1–2 m) and are curved or straight, depending on the species. Oryxes need water more than addaxes and seek streams or waterholes. They will sense and move toward a distant rainstorm. If no water is available, however, they can survive for long periods on dew and vegetation.

The Arabian oryx's white coat (left) reflects the heat of the desert sun. Scimitar-horned oryxes (below) may be extinct in the wild. Successful zoo breeding may allow them to be reintroduced to wildlife preserves in north central Africa.

Avoiding Danger

Closely related to white-tailed deer, mule deer use a different strategy for avoiding danger. Whereas white-tailed deer escape into dense foliage when alarmed, mule deer take cover behind desert rocks or brush.

The Arizona–Sonora Desert Museum has created a natural habitat for mule deer (above and below). The deer's large eyes allow them to detect predators in the dark.

Mule Deer Mule deer flourish in a range of habitats from western North America to Mexico. In the United States, they are found in the Rocky Mountains and in desert regions of the American Southwest. Mule deer average about 3.5 feet (1 m) at the shoulder and have disproportionately large ears. Males grow a new set of antlers each spring. During the summer the antlers may grow half an inch a day.

Mule deer are active primarily in the morning and at dusk. They eat varieties of vegetation, including shrubs, twigs, and farm crops. Desert mule deer obtain most of their water from moist plants and dew. In the driest regions mule deer stay close to water holes. They can run swiftly in rugged terrain. Fawns are born when conditions are best for their survival, usually in the spring.

Over a period of many years, desert bighorn sheep often return to the same spot for sleeping.

Desert Bighorn Sheep

Curly-horned desert bighorn sheep live primarily in the dry, rocky hills and mountain ranges of the American Southwest. They are smaller and lighter in color than Rocky Mountain bighorns. In adapting to a dry climate, desert bighorn sheep have evolved into a distinct subspecies. Though the two subspecies of bighorn sheep can still interbreed, Rocky Mountain bighorns have not adapted for survival in the desert.

Desert bighorn sheep need water every few days but can spend long intervals wandering in dry regions. They graze on grasses, flowers, and dry, thorny bushes such as saltbush and desert holly. They may slice open a barrel cactus with their horns to reach the moist pulp inside. In times of drought, they dig up roots and bulbs with their horns and hooves.

Desert bighorns stay in the home territory of their parents, typically a range of about 10 square miles (25 sq km). For most of the year, males and females travel separately in small herds. Even when vegetation is limited, these animals rarely move beyond their range. They follow known routes through the range, seeking familiar watering places.

A desert bighorn ram (above right) may grow horns weighing up to 25 pounds (12 kg). Female desert bighorn sheep (above left) have short, thin horns that do not curve. Young female bighorns are mature at four years of age; males mature at around seven years of age.

Cold Blood in a Hot Climate

Lizards, snakes, and other reptiles have some advantages as desert dwellers because their scaly skins conserve moisture. As cold-blooded animals, however, their body heat is not internally regulated and they live best at about normal human body temperature. The noonday desert sun would, almost literally, cook them to death. Therefore, many reptiles, particularly snakes, are nocturnal, like other small desert animals, and hunt for food at sunset while the ground is still relatively warm. Some reptiles become torpid at night, meaning that their metabolism slows down as their body temperature falls. In this sluggish condition they consume less energy than when awake and active.

The western diamondback rattlesnake raises its head and shakes its rattle as a warning. More than 200 flexible joints allow the snake to uncoil quickly to strike at prey.

Rattlesnakes Many snakes are found in the deserts of the Americas, but only a few species, mosly rattlesnakes, are poisonous. Rattlesnakes live primarily in the western United States, Mexico, and parts of Central and South America. Some species are not aggressive, but others are easy to provoke. One of the most aggressive is the **western diamondback** rattlesnake of the American Southwest, named for the pattern of its scales.

Rattlesnake venom contains hemotoxins which destroy red blood cells and the walls of blood vessels. The prey die from internal bleeding.

Western diamondbacks usually reach about 5 feet (1.5 m) in length, but some grow to almost 7 feet (2 m). They strike quickly, their folded fangs swinging down and forward. Like all vipers, rattlesnakes have hollow fangs through which they inject deadly venom. The snake does not hold the bite but retreats and waits for the venom to work.

The rattle is made up of segmented rings at the end of the tail. These rings make a buzzing noise when shaken, warning other animals to stay away. When a rattlesnake sheds its skin, the skin at the tip of the tail dries instead of falling off, adding another ring. However, a rattlesnake's age cannot be estimated accurately by counting the rings in its rattle. Some rings may have broken off, or the snake may have shed its skin more frequently than once a year.

Rattlesnakes can detect prey with their flickering tongue or sense vibrations through their bones. They sometimes invade the burrows of kangaroo rats, which try to escape by kicking sand into the snake's eyes or by running to a neighboring burrow.

Desert Snakes

Sand boas use their desert environment to help them capture prey. These snakes bury themselves in the sand with only the tip of their tail showing. They wiggle the tip to attract lizards and rodents. When the prey are within range, the sand boas attack.

The pygmy rattlesnake (top left) and canebrake rattlesnake (below) are two of the 30 rattlesnake species. The blacktail rattlesnake (top right) is relatively harmless, attacking only small rodents as prey.

Lizards Fast or slow moving, colorful or camouflaged, lizards are found in most warm habitats. Though often ferocious in appearance, most species feed on insects and plants and are harmless to humans. They avoid midday heat but otherwise are lively and alert during the day. The deserts of the southwestern United States and Mexico are home to the Gila monster, a poisonous species of beaded lizard. In the same region lives the collared lizard, one of 650 species in the iguana family.

The shy **Gila monster**, rarely seen in the wild, is a stocky lizard about 12 inches (.3 m) long, with shiny scales patterned in black and yellow or black and coral pink. Its colorful scales advertise, rather than hide, its presence to potential predators.

The Gila monster hunts at sunrise in the spring and at night in midsummer. Because it moves slowly, it looks for prey that is immobile or easy to catch, such as insects, eggs, nestlings, or young rodents. If food is scarce, it may retreat to its burrow and live off the fat stored in its tail.

Gila monsters spend most of their time in cool burrows abandoned by other animals. Because they are seldom seen above ground and are nocturnal, Gila monsters were once believed to be rare.

Gila monsters are not aggressive and never bite unless provoked. They use their venom only for defense, not for killing prey. If attacked, a Gila monster bites and locks its jaws like a bulldog, pulling at the victim's flesh until the lizard's venomous saliva seeps into the wound.

In 1952 the Arizona state legislature passed a law protecting Gila monsters. This was the first legal protection ever granted to a venomous species.

Some desert lizards are gray or brown, blending with their habitat, but the **collared lizard** flaunts yellow and turquoise stripes and a distinctive black-and-white neck band. A fast runner, it eats insects and small lizards. Collared lizards can be aggressive, but if threatened are most apt to run quickly away on their hind legs.

Desert lizards, such as the collared lizard, bask on rocks to raise their body temperature. The rocks absorb heat from the sun.

What to look for

Collared lizards have disproportionately large heads and long, thin tails.

Their hind legs are much bigger than their forelegs.

Adult male collared lizards can be recognized by the spots on their throats.

Stingers, Fangs, and Venom

Scorpion

Horned viper

Poisonous animals use their venom in two ways: to defend themselves against predators and to capture food. The horned viper of the Sahara often lies buried in the sand with only its snout protruding, waiting to strike at lizards and rodents. The Egyptian cobra lies in a coil. If disturbed, it rears up, flares its hood, hisses loudly, and strikes.

The venom of both vipers and cobras can be lethal to humans. Cobra venom attacks the nervous system, causing paralysis, while viper venom breaks down red blood cells and causes internal bleeding.

Scorpions, which sting with their tail, are common in deserts. Although some scorpion venom can be lethal to humans, these arachnids sting mainly in self-defense or to stun large and struggling prey. They feed on insects and spiders, and sometimes lizards and mice. Scorpions use their crab-like pincers to seize prey and then arch their tail over their head to sting it.

The hairy black tarantula of the American desert looks frightening, but its venom is relatively harmless to humans. Tarantulas, like all spiders, seize their prey with their fangs, immobilize it with poison, and then digest it externally.

A poisonous mammal, the short-tailed shrew, is found in woodlands and salt marshes of eastern North America. This little animal uses its venomous saliva primarily to kill large insects.

Desert Tortoises Desert tortoises live in the American Southwest and Mexico. Like many other land tortoises, they dig a burrow to escape the daytime heat but emerge briefly early in the morning and at dusk to feed. Unlike other reptiles, tortoises and turtles have no teeth. Instead, their strong jaws are formed into a beak-like shape. Desert tortoises use their beaks to crush leaves and cactus fruit. Moisture-retaining plants are their main sources of water during periods of drought.

After the mating season, the female tortoise buries three to five eggs, which hatch about three months later. Tortoises grow very slowly, and young tortoises, whose shells are soft, are vulnerable to predators. Full-grown desert tortoises average 12 inches (30 cm) in shell length. They are dwarfed by the **Galápagos tortoise**, which, although a member of the same family, may have a shell length of up to 48 inches (122 cm).

The desert tortoise moves at the slow rate of 0.3 miles per hour (0.5 km/h). Members of this endangered species dig horizontal tunnels up to 30 feet (9.1 m) long.

In winter, up to a dozen desert tortoises may hibernate in a large, communal underground den.

Roadrunners such as the California roadrunner are members of the cuckoo family. A roadrunner's call is a series of low notes, *coo coo coo coo-ah coo-ah*, that gradually drop in pitch.

Birds In the Desert

Because birds can fly or run long distances in search of insects, rodents, reptiles or seed-bearing plants, some bird species have adapted to desert life. Birds do not sweat, but ruffle their feathers to cool themselves. Some birds can forage during daytime desert temperatures. Despite these adaptations, some deserts are completely birdless, while other deserts are visited by birds, but not inhabited by them.

Gliding birds such as vultures and falcons escape the heat by soaring thousands of feet into cooler air. Smaller birds, including quail, sparrows, and wrens, take shelter in shady places. Their feathers offer some protection, providing insulation in hot weather as well as cold.

Quail Ground-dwelling quail belong to the same family as pheasants, grouse, and turkeys. They are popular game birds. The **scaled quail**, named for the scalelike patterns on its feathers, is found in the Southwest and Mexico. The **gambel's quail** of the American Southwest is also known as the desert quail.

Roadrunner The roadrunner, a native of the Americas, travels mainly on the ground. A weak flyer because of its short wings, it can run long distances at 13 miles an hour (20 km/h) and sprint for short distances at 25 miles an hour (40 km/h). It skillfully dodges both predators and cars on desert roads.

Roadrunners are large birds, nearly 2 feet (0.6 m) long from beak to tail. Their dark, streaky feathers are offset by pale blue stripes behind their eyes. Their 2-inch (5 cm) crest of head feathers stands erect when they are excited or curious. Roadrunners eat insects, tarantulas, scorpions, snakes—including rattlesnakes—and lizards, which they kill by pounding them on rocks or crushing them with their feet. They can digest most of the flesh, skin, and bones of their prey.

During cold nights roadrunners may save energy by becoming somewhat torpid. In the morning they warm up and preen their feathers in the sun. They nest in twigs that they sometimes bind together with snakeskin and dried cattle or antelope dung.

Roadrunners build a cup-shaped nest in low trees or in clumps of cacti. They line the nest with soft leaves and grass. Female roadrunners lay from two to six eggs.

Both the male (left) and female (right) Anna's hummingbird use their long, thin bills and forked, tubal tongues to get nectar or insects from flowers as they hover. They can also fully rotate their wings.

Hummingbirds' wings may beat as much as 78 times a second. To replace this expended energy, they must consume nearly 2/3 of their body weight in food each day.

Anna's Hummingbird Most North American hummingbirds, named for the humming sound made by their rapidly beating wings in flight, are found in western and southwestern regions. There are several species of tiny hummingbirds, found in forests, semi-deserts, mountains, and even on the edges of suburbia. Anna's hummingbird is less than 4 inches (10 cm) in length, and eats nectar from desert flowers. In cold weather some Anna's hummingbirds migrate in small numbers as far inland as southern Arizona; others winter as far south as Mexico. All return to their home range in the western United States to breed.

Female Anna's hummingbirds are plumed in shades of gray and green. The males are greenish-blue with iridescent, rose-colored heads. Females weave tiny nests out of soft plant fibers and spider's silk and cover the outside with lichen. They lay two white eggs, which require two to three weeks of incubation.

Burrowing Owls Burrowing owls live in both the deserts and dry plains of North and South America. They are relatively small, about 8 to 9 inches (20–22 cm) long, with unusually long legs for running. They can attack prey from the ground or the air. They eat insects, lizards, small birds, rodents, and snakes. They hunt at night, although their day vision is good.

Burrowing owls usually occupy an underground burrow left behind by another digging animal, such as a prairie dog. Sometimes, however, a pair of owls digs a new nest, lining it with dry dung and plant stems.

Sand Grouse Distant relatives of pigeons, sand grouse live principally in the deserts of Africa and Asia. They nest in stony, barren ground far from water and potential predators such as fennec foxes. Sand grouse will fly considerable distances for water, making round-trips of more than 70 miles (115 km).

During the nesting season, the life of a sand grouse becomes even more challenging. The birds must sit on the eggs at all times to prevent them from overheating in the sun. At times they even stand and shade the nest with their wings.

After the eggs hatch, the female remains in the nest while the male sand grouse flies to the nearest waterhole. He drinks and wades in the water, ruffling his feathers until the down becomes saturated. When he returns to the nest his underfeathers are still wet, and the chicks suck water from them. The male sand grouse repeats this trip each day until the chicks are old enough to fly to water themselves.

The burrowing owl (above left) is the only owl that lives in colonies. The elf owl (above right) grows to a mere 6 inches (15 cm). It is the smallest American owl. Chestnut-bellied sandgrouse (below) have feathers that provide camouflage.

Animals of the Deciduous Forest

Deciduous forests consist primarily of trees that shed their leaves each year. As cold or dry weather approaches, deciduous trees, in a bid to conserve moisture, gradually stop replacing the green, energy-absorbing pigment in their leaves. In northern forests, the leaves turn vivid shades of red, yellow, and orange. Seasonal changes also govern the behavior of animals in the deciduous forest. The changes come slowly, allowing animals time to store food for the winter, gain weight, and grow a thick winter coat, or migrate to a warmer climate.

An American black bear forages in an Alaskan woodland.

Animals of the Deciduous Forest

Temperate deciduous forests require 24 to 40 inches (60–100 cm) of annual rainfall and a growing season of 100 to 200 days. Deciduous forests thrive in areas with warm summers and cold winters. Semideciduous forests appear as far south as Central America, where many trees shed their leaves in the dry season.

Unlike tropical forests, which have many different tree species, northern deciduous forests have relatively few. In deciduous forests of the eastern United States a few species, such as red oak, black oak, and shagbark hickory, tend to dominate the forest. In New England, beech, maple, and birch dominate.

Most animals of deciduous forests rely on trees for shelter and food. Birds, deer, and bears eat tree sprouts, seedlings, and fruits. Deer, moose, beavers, and insects eat the leaves. Fallen or hollow trees become dens for raccoons and other animals. In winter, deer, porcupines, and beavers gnaw on tree bark and eat the soft inner layer, which is a good source of vegetable protein in a frozen forest. For all of these animals, trees offer shelter from the wind.

The vivid colors of a deciduous forest in Minnesota signal the change of seasons from summer to autumn.

Amphibians such as salamanders burrow in rotting tree trunks, surfacing to eat insects and worms. Some snakes of the forest prey on small mammals, amphibians, and baby birds.

Most of the animals of the deciduous forest can tolerate cold temperatures. Some grow a thick winter coat; some hibernate in dens or burrows. When hibernating, animals have a slower metabolism and lower body temperature. They survive without eating by drawing on fat reserves.

Some hibernating animals store nuts and seeds underground. Chipmunks, for example, gather as much food as they can, sometimes stuffing as many as six acorns into their cheeks at once for transportation back to their burrow.

Nonhibernating herbivores must adapt to the scarcity of food in winter. One common adaptation is to eat whatever is in season. For example, elk browse on shrubs and conifers that stick up above the snow.

The animals of the deciduous forest are linked together in an intricate food chain. Woodboring insects feed on trees, while ants and beetles consume leaf litter, and mice nibble on seeds and other windfalls on the forest floor. Small mammals are eaten by predators at the top of the food chain such as weasels, bobcats, and cougars. In their competition for food, animals define the boundaries of their territory with scent, urine, calls, mounds of earth, or scrape marks on trees.

Beavers walk slowly and awkwardly on land (top left). A beaver lodge (top right) has a raised sleeping platform shared by the beaver pair and their offspring. Beavers' huge incisors (above) can cut through trees. As their teeth wear down, they grow back.

The Beaver

Eyes are protected by a filmy membrane for swimming.

Nose and ears close up underwater.

Waterproof fur insulates against the cold.

Large, webbed hind feet aid in swimming.

Flat, flexible, scaly tail acts as a powerful propellant in water.

The largest rodents in North America, beavers are found in ponds, lakes, and streams of North America and, in isolated populations, in Eurasia. Their large incisors give them distinctive construction abilities. Their flat, scaly tail is a powerful aid in swimming.

In North America, beavers often create their own ponds, building dams out of sticks, mud, and stones. These ponds serve as a watery habitat for other animals, including otters, muskrats, bullfrogs, and ducks. Beavers also alter the landscape by building canals on which they float logs to

was 750 feet (230 m) long.

Beavers live in lodges made of branches and mud. The lodges are often built away from the shore, forming islands, and can be entered only underwater. The lodge chamber, measuring about 4 feet (1 m) wide by 2 feet (.5 m) high, is insulated by walls a foot thick and ventilated by a small air hole in the roof.

Beavers are herbivores, feeding on leaves, woody stems, and aquatic plants. In cold climates beavers spend the winter in the lodge chamber, feeding on branches they have stored on the muddy floor of the

The Home Range

Large animals such as cougars and bears have a home range, an area in which they normally live and hunt. A home range includes lookout points, water sources, and dens. The animals mark part of their range as a territory and defend it against other animals of the same sex and species. Cougars and wolverines mark their territory with urine; bears leave scrape marks on trees.

The size of a home range depends on topography, the availability of food, and the population density of the species. For example, the home range of a male black bear in Tennessee's Smoky Mountains covers about 16 square miles (41 sq km), but that of a black bear in Idaho, where the climate is harsher and food is less abundant, measures up to 43 square miles (111 sq km).

The size of a range also depends on gender or the season. Female cougars have a home range that averages 15 to 31 square miles (40–80 sq km) and may overlap with that of male cougars, which averages 25 to 35 square miles (65–90 sq km). Most animals wander farthest in the fall, when they must eat to build up fat for winter, and when sexually mature young must find their own territory.

Bears have five long claws on each paw (top) that help them climb trees and mark their territory. As with all bears, American black bears (bottom) have prominent muzzles and a keen sense of smell.

American black bears, such as these in Yellowstone National Park, (left and right), require nearly 20 pounds (9 kg) of food a day. Their diet includes honey, fruit, and other energy-rich foods.

American Black Bear The American black bear is found in both coniferous and deciduous forests as far north as the Arctic Circle and as far south as northern Mexico. It measures no more than three feet (1 m) tall when on all fours but may exceed six feet (2 m) when it rears up on its hind legs. Male black bears average 250 to 350 pounds (115–160 kg). Since brown bears are often twice as heavy as black bears, adults of the two species can be distinguished by their size.

What to look for

American black bears have short tails; most other bears have stumps at the base of the spine.

American black bears may have black, brown, gray, beige, or white fur.

American black bears have a gently tapered muzzle; brown bears have a more disk-shaped muzzle.

Solitary creatures, black bears are most active at night. They try to avoid humans. When traveling near populated areas, bears often walk in streams, which provide dense cover and conceal their scent and tracks. Males will drive other males from their territory but may allow one or more females to stake out smaller territories within theirs. They sometimes stand up on their hind legs in order to see farther or to claw and bite at tree trunks to mark their territory.

Bears occasionally gather in large numbers at prime feeding sites, such as garbage dumps or berry patches. At these times they tend to ignore one another and concentrate on eating.

Black bears are seldom dangerous to people unless they are wounded or their cubs are threatened. When alarmed, they are likely to retreat up a tree. They can run up to 33 miles an hour (53 km/h). Black bears are *omnivores*, meaning that they eat both animals and plants. Depending on availability and season, their diet consists primarily of nuts, berries, and herbs. The remainder may include fish, insects, and carrion.

Asian black bears are sometimes called moon bears because of the crescent-shaped patch of white hair on their chests (left). Long, shaggy fur covers their neck and shoulders (right).

Asian Black Bear Found from Iran through the Himalayas to Korea and Japan, the Asian black bear is of the same family as the American black bear but of a different genus. It tends to be a little smaller than the American black bear—the maximum size of a male is about 265 pounds (120 kg). Asian black bears are usually black but may be brown or reddish–brown.

Asian black bears' home range, often in mountainous regions, may cover as little as 2 square miles (5 sq km). They are good climbers, eating and resting on tree platforms made from broken branches.

Like American black bears, Asian black bears are omnivorous but feed mainly on plants. Primarily nocturnal, they will sometimes search for favorite ripening fruits during the day. Like most species of bears, Asian black bears love honey and often raid wild bees' nests, ignoring the bee stings. They rarely attack livestock but can kill a domestic cow by breaking its neck. In cold regions they sleep during the winter; in warm regions their hibernation period is shorter or omitted altogether.

The cougar, like all big cats, has excellent vision. Cougars can see six times better than humans in dim light. Cougars can jump as much as 20 feet (7 m) in a single leap.

The cougar's vocalizations range from a quiet whistle to a loud scream.

Cougar Cougars once lived throughout the Americas. In different regions of the United States people assigned them different names: cougar, mountain lion, puma, panther, and catamount—all the same species of big, tawny cat. After centuries of being hunted, cougars are now found mainly in western North America, where they live in various habitats, including both forests and plains. Adult male cougars weigh up to 225 pounds (100 kg); females are somewhat smaller.

Unless they are mating, cougars are solitary and secretive. Active at night, they move quietly on heavily padded paws. They put their hind paws in the prints made by their front paws to muffle the sound. Cougars stalk and then pounce on their prey, breaking the animal's neck or clamping its windpipe shut until it suffocates. They usually prey on large hoofed animals but will eat almost any mammal when they are hungry, including porcupines. Searching for such big game as deer, elk, and bighorn sheep, they sometimes travel 20 to 25 miles (32–40 km) in a day.

Cougar kittens begin to hunt with their mother when only two months old. During their second year, they leave their mother's home range to find ranges of their own.

Like all cats, cougars run on their toes. This helps them make sudden turns and keep their balance.

A White Flag

If white-tailed deer hear a sound while feeding, they look up anxiously and perk up their ears. If the sound is repeated, they give a snort of alarm and dash away, holding their tail erect like a white flag. This white marker helps fawns follow their mother through a dark forest. From a distance it may serve as a danger signal to other deer.

White-tailed deer have slender, powerful legs that enable them to flee quickly from predators. They also use them to trample and kill snakes.

White-Tailed Deer White-tailed deer are found throughout much of the Americas in habitats that include deserts and tropical forests as well as deciduous forests. Although there is only one species of white-tailed deer, there are many local subspecies, which vary greatly in size. In northern, cooler regions, white-tailed deer tend to be large. Northern bucks generally weigh 200 to 300 pounds (90–135 kg). At the other extreme, key deer, a tiny subspecies of white-tailed deer found in the Florida Keys, weigh only about 50 pounds (23 kg).

The home range of a white-tailed deer varies, from 60 to 150 acres (25–60 ha) for a female and from 240 to 880 acres (97–355 ha) for a male. They may wander a mile or two during their daily search for grass, twigs, mushrooms, fruit, nuts, and lichens. In common with some other even-toed animals, such as bison and antelope, deer are ruminants and chew their cud. (See "Ruminants," p. 89.)

White-tailed deer have become adapted to live near the plentiful shrubs and low vegetation of pasturelands and suburbs. Some people with gardens consider deer a nuisance.

Scent glands on their haunches, ankles, and hooves play an important role in communication among white-tailed deer. With every step, scent seeps from between their hooves, laying down an invisible path that enables deer to find one another or to retrace their steps. Large amounts of the same musky scent are discharged as a warning when deer are alarmed. Males in rut also give off a strong scent. Males can determine when females are ready to mate by the scent of their urine or by the smell of the ground where they have been lying.

What to look for

Stag elk's spreading antlers may measure more than 5 feet (1.5 m) across.

Stag elk are considered mature when each antler has six points.

Both stags and does have the same sleek coats as red deer; in winter they both grow dark manes.

Elk After moose, elk are the largest members of the deer family. A bull elk may weigh half a ton (450 kg). Elk were once the most widely distributed species of deer in North America. Intensive hunting and habitat destruction reduced their numbers until by 1900 there were only about 40,000 left. Conservation efforts have increased the population to about half a million. Elk are found in the largest numbers in the Rocky Mountains, the Pacific Northwest, and Canada.

Elk live in a variety of habitats where they can find twigs, shrubs, and other vegetation. They receive much of the moisture they need from their diet but also drink from springs and lakes, and in winter will eat snow. To keep away from flies in hot weather, they sometimes sleep on snowbanks.

Stag elk usually gain an additional tine on their antlers each time they grow back.

Elk herds are segregated by gender except during the breeding season. Stags live in all-male groups of five or six animals in the spring and summer but join mixed herds in winter to migrate to ranges where the snow is less deep. Older stags occasionally remain behind on the northerly parts of their range, even though heavy snow may hinder their movement and leave them vulnerable to predators.

After the young are born, mothers and calves leave the herd for several weeks. Calves usually weigh 30 to 40 pounds (14–18 kg) at birth and can follow their mothers when three days old. After one month they begin to graze, although they continue to nurse for four to seven months. As the calves grow stronger, the mothers and young create herds, which increase in size over the summer and may number more than five hundred.

More than 8,000 American elk live under protection at the National Elk Refuge in Wyoming.

Stag elk sometimes lock antlers while fiercely fighting for access to fertile females during rut.

When only two to four weeks old, a baby skunk can point its tail toward an intruder and spray scent.

The black and white markings on the coat of this striped skunk warn other animals to keep their distance. Skunks with prominent markings have the most potent spray. In North America, wild skunks are a major carrier of rabies.

Keeping Predators at a Distance

Skunks and porcupines, two animals found in deciduous forests, employ unusual defense strategies. The acrid scent of a skunk discourages most predators, except those near starvation. Porcupines are attacked more often, but would-be predators often retreat with a muzzle full of quills and an empty stomach.

Skunks The most common species of skunks found in parts of North and Central America are the **striped skunk** and the **spotted skunk**. Members of the weasel family, these black-and-white creatures have become adapted to many environments, including cities. Some skunks forage at night for garbage. The long, curved claws on their front feet are also useful for digging up grubs and for pouncing on mice and grasshoppers.

In northern latitudes skunks spend most of the winter sleeping, though their metabolism does not slow down enough for them to be considered true hibernators. For their burrow, skunks usually use holes abandoned by other animals or natural cavities such as hollow logs.

If provoked, skunks react by arching their back and sometimes hissing or clicking their teeth. If the adversary does not retreat, skunks quickly lift their tail and bend over, pointing their backside at the target while looking over their shoulders. Skunks have good aim and can spray a noxious discharge from their anal glands 9 to 16 feet (3–5 m). Smaller-sized spotted skunks are generally livelier than striped skunks and are more aggressive toward enemies. Spotted skunks do a handstand on their front legs when discharging scent.

A porcupine's sharp quills deter all predators except the cougar, the wolverine, and the fisher, a large member of the weasel family. These predators can flip a porcupine on its back and attack its soft, unquilled belly.

Porcupines Porcupines are the second-largest North American rodent after beavers. The **American porcupine** is found in both deciduous and coniferous forests of North America and as far south as northern Mexico.

Stocky, short-legged, and nearsighted, porcupines weigh up to 16 pounds (7 kg). One porcupine may have as many as 30,000 quills, each quill about 3 inches (8 cm) long, covering nearly all the exposed parts of its body except its nose and belly.

Porcupines are solitary, slow-moving, non-aggressive animals. If cornered on the ground, however, they will hide their head and turn their back, erecting their quills and lashing out with their muscular tail. Porcupines cannot actually "throw" their quills; rather, the quills detach easily when they come in contact with another animal. One lash of a porcupine's tail can drive quills deep into a predator's flesh.

In winter, porcupines are less active. They survive on bark and pine needles and often kill trees by girdling them, or eating a ring around their trunk. In spring they eat young birds, leaves, willow blossoms, and other vegetation. They get essential nutrients, such as calcium, by gnawing on animal bones or discarded antlers. In addition, they may lick the dried sweat on canoe paddles or horse harnesses to obtain salt, which is harder to find.

American porcupines do not roam far from their shelters during the winter. In the summer their range averages 36 acres (15 ha).

Because their hollow quills give them buoyancy, porcupines are good swimmers.

Feeding Time at the Zoo

Feeding baby tiger

Commissary

Live crickets

Hand-feeding stringbeans to rhinos

Meeting the nutritional needs of zoo animals is a massive undertaking. Menus must be carefully designed to follow each animal's natural diet as closely as possible. Foods must be analyzed for fiber, fat, and mineral contents. At the zoo commissary, or kitchen, large quantities of both ordinary and specialized foods must be stored, prepared, and delivered promptly. Early morning is the busiest feeding time. Zoo animals are frequently fed in separate enclosures to ensure that each animal eats its own food. This also allows zookeepers to check how much each animal eats.

Food is presented to animals in ways that encourage natural behavior. Tigers and leopards, for example, receive large chunks of meat, big bones, or whole chickens so they can rip and tear at their food as they would in the wild.

Since chimpanzees and other primates forage for food in their natural habitat, zookeepers hide raisins and sunflower seeds in the grass and tree holes of their enclosures. Leafy branches are hung from tall trees so that giraffes can browse as they would on the African savanna.

In the rare event that an infant animal is orphaned or abandoned by its mother, it is fed by zoo veterinarians or in a zoo nursery. The fat and carbohydrate needs of baby animals differ considerably: some animals are fed commercial baby food; others require specially formulated liquids. Baby birds need careful monitoring—some

Hand-feeding squid to seals

Food trays

Water dragon eating mouse

...n with bone

fledglings are fed as frequently as every few minutes.

Feeding thousands of animals is an expensive undertaking. The National Zoo in Washington, D.C. is a case in point. It spends more than $500,000 a year on groceries, which include 715,000 live crickets, 150,000 fish, 400 tons (362,800 kg) of hay, 65,000 tomatoes, and many other items.

Every day, a single elephant eats 100 pounds (45 kg) of hay and another 30 pounds (14 kg) of fruits and vegetables. An adult python eats only once every three weeks but can eat 20 rats at one meal.

Much of what zoo animals eat is the same as what humans eat. The apples and oranges, vegetables, and fresh fish provided at the zoo are the same as those

found in a grocery store. An elephant's diet, for example, includes bread, eggs, dry cereal, honey, and applesauce.

The average zoo menu contains some notable differences, however. In addition to live crickets, special-ordered from a cricket farm, there are blackworms, red-worms, night crawlers, guppies, and meal-worms. When available, dead lizards and mice are also served to snakes and birds.

Storing tons of food is also a challenge. Most major zoos keep bulk supplies in huge warehouses equipped with walk-in refrigerators and freezers.

Some zoos grow their own specialized food. The San Diego Zoo harvests eucalyptus leaves for koalas, hibiscus for leaf-eating monkeys, and acacia for giraffes.

Before winter sets in, a raccoon (left) develops a thick layer of fat beneath its fur to conserve heat. Strong hind legs and a long tail support a raccoon's weight so that its front paws are free to seize and handle food (right).

At Home in the Trees

Raccoons There are six species of raccoons, only one of which lives in North America, the **common raccoon**. The common raccoon is now also found in Europe and Asia where it was introduced. Adult common raccoons weigh between 15 and 44 pounds (7–20 kg), with the largest found in northern latitudes.

Resistant to rain and snow, a raccoon's coat is made up of dense, woolly underfur and long guard hairs. The coat is shed once a year, falling out gradually over the spring and summer. For this reason, raccoons sometimes appear slightly ragged in summer. Raccoons look sleek and glossy in the fall, when their coat is at its fullest.

Raccoons usually live near lakes and streams, where they can catch crayfish, frogs, turtles, and small fish. With short curved claws they dig up turtle eggs, open mussels, and pull apart logs. Raccoons also eat mice, eggs, berries, nuts, and insects. Though most active at night, raccoons are sometimes seen foraging in suburban areas during the day. Raccoons den in hollow trees with entrances at least 10 feet (3 m) above the ground.

What to look for

Raccoons have circles of black hair around their eyes—sometimes called a "mask."

A raccoon's bushy, ringed tail, grows up to 15 inches (38 cm) in length.

Raccoons have five curved, nonretractable toes on each foot.

Opossums The excellent survival instincts of opossums, the only marsupial in the Americas, have helped them adapt to human-dominated habitats as successfully as raccoons. The **Virginia opossum** is found primarily in wooded areas of North America. The **mouse opossum** lives in the tropical forests of Latin America. The only aquatic marsupial, the **water opossum** is found in freshwater rivers and lakes from southern Mexico to northern Argentina. The smallest species of opossum, the **Formosan mouse opossum,** measures less than 3 inches (7 cm) in head-body length. The Virginia opossum measures up to 20 inches (55 cm) in head-body length.

As an innate response to danger, an opossum becomes immobile, seeming to be dead, or "playing possum." In this trancelike state its heart rate slows and its breathing becomes shallow, even stopping for as long as 30 seconds. Because the animal appears to be dead, some predators will then leave it alone.

Opossums have a scaly, prehensile tail that is used for balance when eating. They also use the tail to carry grass to their nest for bedding. Adult opossums seldom hang by the tail except in an emergency. However, baby opossums have a stronger tail in proportion to their body weight than adults do and use it to keep from falling. Opposable thumbs on the hind feet are useful for climbing.

Opossums eat a varied diet of snails, worms, seeds, fruit, and carrion. Their eyes are adapted for nocturnal foraging, but they rely primarily on their keen senses of smell and hearing. Predators include coyotes, wolves, and great horned owls.

Opossums, such as the Chilean mouse opossum (top), have a pointed snout and sensitive whiskers. Female Virginia opossums (below) can have more than 50 young in a litter, but many do not survive the journey from the birth canal to the pouch.

The American kestrel is the only small falcon with a reddish-brown back and tail. Female kestrels are slightly larger than males.

Food for the Birds

Because temperate deciduous forests are rich in insects, rodents, nuts, seeds, and berries, they are also rich in bird life. Some birds, such as a few species of wood warblers, nest in immature forests. Most birds, however, flourish best in forests where trees are not harvested for timber but instead are allowed to grow old, fall to the ground, and decay. In such forests, about one–quarter of the insects live in rotting logs and branches. Woodpeckers extract beetle larvae from the bark crevices of living trees, helping to keep the trees healthy. Other birds, such as American kestrels, fly beyond the forest's edge in search of food.

American kestrel The American kestrel, or **sparrowhawk**, is a small falcon with a wingspread of 8 inches (20 cm) or less. It nests at the edges of forests and preys upon both forest and grasslands animals. Kestrels often hunt over open land where, like kingfishers or ospreys, they can hover and dive for their prey unhindered by branches. They live mainly on large insects such as grasshoppers, but also eat small snakes, lizards, birds, and rodents.

The courtship of two kestrels begins when the male stages dramatic dives and then brings food to the female. After mating, kestrels often nest in hollow trees or in woodpecker holes, evicting existing tenants if necessary.

Some woodpecker species have a tongue 4 inches (10 cm) long. It retracts into an internal casing that curves around the back of the skull.

Woodpeckers Most of the 209 species of woodpeckers nest in forests and are highly adapted to tree life. However, woodpeckers can also be found in many other habitats, from tundra to deserts. When searching a tree for insects, they work their way upward, clinging with their clawed toes and propping themselves with their long, stiff tail feathers. Listening for burrowing insects, they use their beak to hammer into an insect's tunnel, and extract their prey with their long tongue. Their barbed tongue is coated with sticky saliva.

The pileated woodpecker is the largest species of woodpecker in North America, growing nearly 17 inches (45 cm) in length. It can be recognized by its raised red crest and very loud *wuck-a-wuck-a* call.

Both males and females drum with their bills on trees to declare their territory and to attract a mate. Each species of woodpecker has its own particular drumming or tapping patterns. Woodpeckers also often drum on dead or dry branches, which are more resonant and produce a sharper sound than living trees. The crow-sized European **black woodpecker** drums 500 to 600 times a day during the breeding season, pounding at the rate of 6 to 10 strokes a second in bursts that are repeated 10 times a minute. The much smaller **pied woodpecker** is even faster, striking the wood 12 to 14 times in less than a second.

What to look for

Woodpeckers have two toes that point forward and two that point backward on each foot for climbing tree trunks.

Most male woodpeckers have larger red markings than females.

Marsupials

Tree kangaroo

Koala and cub

Opossum in pouch

Opossum and young

Marsupials are mammals with pouches in females for their young. Tiny newborn marsupials make their way to the pouch, staying there while they complete early development. Nipples in the pouch enable the young to nurse.

Although there are about 250 species of marsupials, only one, the Virginia opossum, is native to North America. In Australia, however, marsupials are the predominant mammals. Most marsupials are herbivores, but a few of the species, such as the

Tasmanian devil, are carnivores.

Marsupials show a wide range of adaptive behavior. Wombats do not sweat or drink water, and are among the burrowing marsupials that have successfully adapted to the Australian desert. Feathertail gliders, tiny members of the opossum family, live in Australian forests. Membranes stretched between ankle and wrist on either side of their body enable the feathertail gliders to use air currents and to glide up to 65 feet (20 m) from one tree to another.

Red kangaroo and joey in pouch

Spotted tiger quoll

Tasmania

Kangaroos are probably the best-known Australian marsupial. The common red kangaroo feeds on the grasses of its habitat; the gray kangaroo forages on forest plants as well. The hill kangaroo, like the wombat, has become adapted to dry terrain.

The koala is another Australian marsupial. It has only a stump for a tail, but its sharp, opposing claws are adapted to grip the branches of eucalyptus trees. Male koalas average 23 pounds (10.5 kg), nearly twice the weight of females.

Mainly nocturnal, leaves of certain euca and sometimes the lea branches of a given tr them difficult to rais supplement their diet tains necessary nutrie Females give birth to c

Early European sett millions of koalas for t ance and forest fires r Koalas are now a prot

Animals of the Coniferous Forest

In coniferous forests winter can last as long as eight months. In this harsh climate there is less disturbance from humans than in deciduous forests. Creatures such as wolves, lynx, and brown bears—which have been hunted to extinction in southern parts of their former range—live and multiply among the quiet, snowy pines and spruces of the north.

Grazing on open ground or in woodlands, caribou are found from western Alaska to western Greenland.

The Vast Northern Forest

Northern coniferous forests, also known as *boreal* forests or *taiga*, lie primarily in the northern temperate zone, which begins at roughly 55° north latitude and extends in a few places to the edge of the Arctic Circle. These forests stretch in a wide band covering more than 6,000 miles (10,000 km) from Alaska through Canada to the Atlantic coast, and from Scandinavia through Siberia to the Bering Strait. Coniferous forests are composed largely of conifers, or evergreens, trees that produce seeds carried in cones. Conifers also grow in parts of the Southern Hemisphere and on some mountain ranges, where they replace deciduous forests at varying altitudes.

Evergreen needles are so waxy and bitter that only a few animals eat them.

Because of their shorter growing season, coniferous forests, such as this one in the state of Washington, have less diverse plant life than deciduous forests.

Conifer cones are either male or female, the female cones producing seeds. Many deciduous trees, such as maple and birch, invest much energy in producing flowers, nuts, or seeds each year. Conifers, however, take two or three years to produce a single crop of cones. The narrow, waxy needles of most conifers conserve water more effectively than the broader leaves of deciduous trees. By retaining their needles through winter, conifers can begin photosynthesis as soon as the temperature reaches 52°F (11°C), thus taking maximum advantage of a short growing season.

Pine cones, which litter the forest floor in abundant supply in some years, are an essential first link in the food chain of the coniferous forest. Both red squirrels and birds, such as crossbills and grosbeaks, feed on pine cone seeds. The cone seeds discarded by squirrels and birds become food for rodents such as mice and lemmings, which have frequent, large litters. (A lemming can mate when it is only 19 days old, have 12 young in a litter, and breed 3 times in a season). These prolific rodents are, in turn, a primary food source for predatory mammals and birds such as owls and hawks. Even large carnivores such as wolves and grizzly bears prey on rodents when other food is scarce.

Familiar Faces in Remote Regions

The animals of the coniferous forest have an extremely wide geographic range. The brown bear, the gray wolf, the lynx, the wolverine, the caribou, and the moose are the same individual species in both North America and Eurasia. Although there are regional size differences, a moose browsing in Maine is the same species as a valley moose in northern China. A wolverine burrowing in Finland is the same species as a wolverine foraging in Montana. Although they are known by different names, the first reindeer domesticated in Eurasia almost three thousand years ago are actually the same species as North American caribou.

During the winter, animals such as this female moose must dig through the snow to find food.

Gray Wolf Until a few centuries ago, the gray wolf had the widest range of any living terrestrial mammal except humans. The gray wolf is still found in the vast coniferous forests of the former Soviet Union, in Canada, and in parts of the northern United States. The only other species of wolf, the **red wolf**, inhabits the southeastern United States. Gray wolves vary in size from region to region. Those found in warm climates may weigh as little as 26 pounds (12 kg) and stand only 2 feet (60 cm) tall at the shoulder. In the colder climates of North America and Russia, gray wolves may weigh up to 120 pounds (55 kg) and stand almost 3 feet (1 m) tall at the shoulder.

All domestic dogs are descended from the gray wolf, which was probably first tamed in southern Asia about 13,000 years ago.

In spite of their name, gray wolves range in color from white to black. The shade of their coat is often adapted to the local environment. They grow a thick, long coat in fall and winter, and shed it in spring. Their claws are blunt, but wolves have sharp teeth and powerful jaws for tearing flesh and cracking bones. They have an excellent sense of smell and have been known to scent a caribou nearly 2 miles (3 km) away. They also locate prey by following tracks in the snow.

Before lying down, gray wolves walk in a circle, flattening the leaves and grass beneath them. Domestic dogs perform a similar ritual, even where there are no leaves or grass to flatten.

Wolf Rank and Behavior

A Red wolf

Many animals communicate through vocalization and physical behavior. Social animals such as wolves use a variety of signals to indicate status within their group.

- **Bowing** A submissive wolf may lower its body and put its tail between its legs.
- **Growling** A wolf may signify dominance by growling and raising its hackles.
- **Staring** Holding its back rigid and its tail stiffly extended, one wolf may dominate another by staring it down.
- **Licking** A submissive wolf may allow its tongue to hang out, and may even lick the dominant wolf's mouth.
- **Mounting** A dominant wolf may stand on its back legs and put its paws on the other wolf's shoulders, often while growling or appearing to bite.

In summer wolves hunt at night, but in winter they may be active during the day. Moving in single file along roads, trails, or frozen streams, they can cover up to 125 miles (200 km) in a day. Wolves howl—when separated from the pack or to announce the pack's territorial claims—in an eerie cacophony that can be heard 7 miles (10 km) away. Wolf packs usually hunt large animals, such as deer, moose, and caribou, though individuals may catch smaller prey. A wolf can eat 20 pounds (9 kg) of meat at a time.

Wolves gear most of their activities to the needs of the pack, which consists of a dominant pair, their pups, and other adults. Most packs have eight or fewer adult members. Occasionally another male will successfully fight the dominant male for control of the pack. Most of the time wolves reinforce their rank by their behavior. For example, the dominant wolves in a pack eat first, before allowing the subdominant wolves to feed.

Each member of a wolf pack howls at a different pitch. Timber wolf is a common name given to gray wolves that live in forests.

The Lynx

Ear tufts for sharper hearing

Brownish–gray coat for camouflage

Relatively long legs for traveling through deep snow

Footpads covered by dense fur for traveling through snow

In danger of extinction, lynx are hunted for their beautiful pelts. They are also destroyed as pests because they sometimes kill domestic animals.

The North American lynx stalks prey alone. When prey is plentiful, lynx often hunt in groups.

Lynx A member of the cat family, the lynx is now extinct in most of the United States and Europe but is still widespread in the coniferous forests of Canada and Eurasia. This solitary cat inhabits dense, remote forests and rarely ventures into open country.

North American lynx weigh up to 35 pounds (15 kg) and are only about twice the size of a domestic tomcat. Eurasian lynx are larger, some weighing 85 pounds (40 kg). All lynx have keen eyesight and excellent hearing.

Primarily nocturnal, lynx hunt hares, deer, mice, and birds. They depend especially on snowshoe hares as food, and their population tends to rise and fall with the hare population.

Lynx do not rely on speed to capture their prey. Instead, they use their excellent stalking skills, approaching prey to within a few bounds. They also lie in ambush until prey comes near, hiding by flattening themselves on a ledge or tree limb. Although they are agile climbers and good swimmers, lynx are surprisingly slow on the ground. A dog can easily run down a lynx, though it faces a fierce, snarling opponent at the end of the chase.

Rarely seen even in regions where they are common, lynx, (as well as mountain lions and tigers), have been known to track a solitary human hiker for hours out of apparent curiosity. The cause of this behavior is not known.

European lynx (below), like most cats, are very protective mothers. Their young resemble domestic cats or kittens.

Bears of the North

Brown Bear The most widely distributed bear in the world, all brown bears belong to a single species. Subspecies include the **grizzly bear** of North America, named for the grizzled, or gray-streaked, fur on its back and shoulders, and the **Kodiak bear** of coastal Alaska, which is the largest brown bear, weighing up to 1,800 pounds (800 kg) and standing up to 10 feet (3 m) tall on its hind legs.

Most brown bears weigh between 350 and 700 pounds (150–300 kg). Females tend to be smaller than males. Brown bears have a massive head, powerful jaws, humped shoulders, and long claws. Some are brown, but others are black, reddish, or blond.

Brown bears can run up to 40 miles an hour (65 km/h), fast enough to catch a galloping horse and knock it down with a swipe of the paw. Their sense of smell is as keen as a bloodhound's. An extraordinary homing ability enables them to find their home territory even after being captured and released 100 miles (160 km) away. When brown bears are pursued, they often try to cover their tracks.

Brown bears, such as the Kodiak (above), use their long claws to dig for bulbs and rodents. Grizzly bears (below) eat meat, but survive mostly on greens and tuberous vegetables such as carrots.

Brown bears, like most bears, are omnivores, and their diet varies according to their environment. Some, such as the **Japanese brown bear**, are herbivores, eating bulbs, roots, grasses, mushrooms, nuts, and berries. Brown bears in the Canadian Rockies will hunt moose, elk, mountain sheep, and even black bears. Black bears can escape from brown bears by climbing trees, since the long foreclaws of brown bears are not adapted for climbing. When salmon are migrating upstream, brown bears spend much of the day fishing, catching the fish in their jaws or pinning them between their forepaws.

Hibernation is a response to cold weather and dwindling food supplies. Because they are fed regularly, bears in zoos usually do not hibernate.

During late summer and early fall brown bears may eat 80 to 90 pounds (35–40 kg) of food in one day. In winter, they hibernate in a low cave, a hollow tree, or an underground den, insulating the chamber with dry leaves and grasses. Bears can be easily awakened from hibernation but, if not disturbed, they may sleep for as long as a month without changing position.

Like black bears (see pp. 129, 134–135), female brown bears give birth during hibernation, having mated in late spring or early summer. The fertilized egg does not implant in the wall of the uterus until much later, usually in the fall, and then only if the female is well nourished and healthy. Newborn brown bears weigh only 10 ounces (280 g), a tiny baby for a 450-pound (200 kg) mother. The average litter is two cubs. When the family leaves the den in the spring, the mother must fiercely defend her cubs from predation by male bears and wolves.

This Kodiak bear will carry its salmon catch out of the water and then carefully strip off the skin and flesh. Bears do not eat the head, the tail, or the bones of fish.

Following a Seasonal Diet

Carnivores such as wolves and lynx eat fresh meat year-round, though prey is often more scarce during the winter. Herbivores, however, must adapt their diet to whatever plants are available in a particular season. In winter, when small bushes and herbs are covered with snow and deciduous trees lose their leaves, moose, caribou, and other members of the deer family (see pp. 162–165) must eat twigs and dig in the snow to uncover moss, lichens, and other green plants.

Moose Moose, all of which belong to one species, are found in deciduous and coniferous forests throughout the world. The largest member of the deer family, moose may measure 7 feet (2 m) tall at the shoulder and weigh up to 1,500 pounds (700 kg). Large, flat antlers may measure more than 6 feet (2 m) from tip to tip.

Moose can run up to 35 miles an hour (60 km/h). Their long legs enable them to walk through snow up to 3 feet (1 m) deep. Though usually solitary, they sometimes form herds during harsh winter weather. In deep snow they gather among sheltering trees to trample the snow and feed on twigs and bark. This tactic enables moose to share body heat and keep mutual watch for

Moose are often found near water (left and right) where they eat large amounts of sodium-rich aquatic plants.

predators such as wolves. Moose are near-sighted and have been known to charge people who come within close range.

Moose eat bark, gouging willows and aspens by cutting the bark upward with their lower teeth. They rear up on their hind legs to browse on conifer branches that are almost out of reach. To maintain their weight, moose must eat up to 60 pounds (30 kg) of vegetation each day.

Strong swimmers, moose can hold their breath underwater for a minute or more. They wade into lakes and streams in late spring and summer to feed on aquatic plants such as waterlilies, and to avoid being bitten by insects.

In spring, moose shed their thick, dull winter coat and grow a new coat of reddish-brown hair, which is lustrous and almost black by late summer. Like other deer, bull moose begin to grow velvet-covered antlers in the spring.

In the former Soviet Union, moose are bred for their milk and meat. They are also sometimes used as pack animals.

What to look for

Moose have a large, elongated head and a broad, flat nose.

Male moose have flabby, bell-shaped skin hanging from their throat.

Moose appear to be humped because their back is lower at the rump.

Because they have few predators, moose, such as this female (below), can browse slowly on energy-providing plants.

A male caribou pauses to graze and drink in an Alaskan forest.

Caribou There is only one species of caribou, also called reindeer, and its geographic range is extensive. In arctic regions of Eurasia and North America, wild caribou are often herded and trained for domestic use. In addition to meat production, they are used as both pack animals and sleigh pullers by the nomadic Sami (Lapps) of northern Scandinavia.

Caribou are medium-sized deer, weighing 200 to 600 pounds (100–300 kg). Their splayed, concave hooves are ideal for traveling over snowy and boggy ground. They have a keen sense of smell and can detect plants buried under more than 6 inches (15 cm) of snow. A well-furred muzzle protects them from frostbite while they are feeding.

A caribou's coat, brownish in summer and grizzled in winter, offers excellent insulation. In common with many arctic mammals, the caribou's coat has long guard hairs to protect the thick, soft wool underneath and ensure that the animals stay dry even during a sleet storm. The effect is like wearing a waterproof parka over a thick wool sweater. This insulation serves caribou well when they plunge into lakes and rivers during migrations or when they flee predators. Like moose, caribou conserve heat during the harshest part of the winter by huddling together under the protective canopy of evergreens.

Caribou gather in large herds composed of both cows and immature bulls. Mature bulls usually stay apart in small bands of their own. Herds of tundra caribou may number up to

Female caribou (above and below) have smaller, less ornate antlers than male caribou. As caribou walk, a slipping tendon in each foot makes a distinct clicking sound.

Caribou calves can follow their mother one hour after birth, and can outrun a human when they are one day old.

500,000 animals. They migrate up to 600 miles (950 km) each year, moving from northern forests to open tundra in the spring and back to the forests in the fall. Herds provide protection against wolves, which are the caribou's constant followers. In summer, caribou eat as much as they can. They need the extra fat to nourish them in winter.

During the breeding season, or *rut*, the neck of an adult bull swells and his mane thickens, showing white against the deep brown of his body. Newborn calves weigh 10 to 20 pounds (5–9 kg). A few months after birth, two bony knobs appear on the skull of both male and female calves. In the first year these develop into small, spiked antlers, which reach their full size by the third year. Caribou live about $4\frac{1}{2}$ years in the wild but up to 20 years in zoos.

Fearless Hunters in the Snow

To both predator and prey, wolverines are formidable adversaries. Although rarely attacked by a lone predator, the fearless wolverine is occasionally overcome by packs of animals, such as wolves.

Wolverine The shaggy, blackish-brown wolverine is the largest member of the weasel family, a large, varied group of mammals called *mustelids*. The wolverine is a single species found in the coniferous forests and the tundra of northern Eurasia and North America, roaming over home ranges that may cover 250 square miles (650 sq km). A stocky animal, it measures only about 3 feet (1 m) from head to tail and weighs 25 to 70 pounds (10–30 kg), but it is extremely strong and aggressive for its size.

Though wolverines spend most of their time on the ground, they are agile climbers and will retreat up a tree if threatened. Their claws are sharp, and their jaws are powerful enough to crush thick bones.

Tireless in a chase, wolverines can run up to 40 miles (65 km) at a time. Their broad paws and splayed toes are adapted for running on soft snow. In winter they can catch larger and heavier prey, such as caribou and elk, that would outrun them on dry ground. A wolverine will leap on the back of a fleeing caribou and bite its neck, riding it before bringing it down. During summer, when they can no longer outrun hoofed animals, wolverines eat berries, eggs, young birds, lemmings, carrion, and, occasionally, young caribou or porcupines.

Wolverines can protect their kills from bears and cougars. Their keen sense of smell also enables them to locate carrion left by other predators. Occasionally they bury extra meat in the snow and may return to these caches up to six months later.

Wolverines are solitary except during the spring and summer breeding season. In midwinter the female digs a den in a deep snowdrift and gives birth to a litter of two to four offspring. The young remain with the mother through the summer. In late fall the young adults must seek a new territory, often moving 20 to 60 miles (30–100 km) from their birthplace.

Wolverines are now rare in the wild. They have been ruthlessly hunted for their pelts and killed by farmers to protect livestock.

Conserving Heat in a Cold Climate

To survive in harsh conditions, warm-blooded animals must maintain a constant body temperature. Animals living in cold climates have thick, waterproof fur that keeps heat near the body, and chilling ice and snow away from it. Feathers provide similar insulation for birds.

Large animals, such as moose, deer, and walrus, have layers of insulating fat under the skin. This fat can be converted into energy when food is scarce.

Adaptations of body size and shape also help conserve heat. Animals with round bodies, and large animals with short limbs, have less surface area in proportion to their body size than tall, slender animals. This means that a smaller part of the animal's body is exposed to the cold.

Ear size is another adaptation to living in a cold climate. Arctic foxes and rabbits have much smaller ears than their relatives in the desert. Small ears have less surface area to lose heat, and are compact and close to the body.

Adaptations in behavior also help animals survive during the winter. While hunting, an animal cannot expend more energy in the chase than it will replenish from eating its prey. Therefore, a wolf can spend a long time chasing a deer but not a rabbit. Hunting in packs also helps to conserve energy. When a wolf pack chases a deer, each wolf expends less energy than if it were chasing the deer alone.

Bats, woodchucks, and some other animals conserve energy through hibernation, a sleeplike state of dormancy during which heart rate, breathing rate, and body temperature are lowered. Most warm-blooded hibernators, such as bears and rodents, arouse themselves occasionally to feed.

Finally, some animals, such as birds and caribou, avoid harsh winter conditions by migrating to warmer areas.

Martens Widely dispersed in many regions of Europe and North America, martens are also members of the weasel family. Heavier than most weasels, martens have golden-brown, black, or yellow fur. Curious by nature and susceptible to the bait placed in traps, martens are easy for hunters to trap.

Martens are tree climbers and have familiar pathways along branches and through treetops as well as on the ground. They use their bushy tail for balance as they leap from branch to branch. Their climbing ability keeps them safe from most predators, but martens are occasionally caught by red foxes, lynx, cougars, and great horned owls.

The **American marten**, or **American pine marten**, has large paws and can run on top of the snow, though it is more apt to burrow for prey. It hunts mice, squirrels, rabbits, and grouse by searching brush piles and crevices or by tunneling under the snow near fallen logs and tree stumps. The **fisher** is another species of North American marten.

Martens are usually solitary. They do not hibernate but continue to hunt all winter, staying in their den only in very cold or wet weather. In mountainous areas they may move to lower elevations during the winter where they can take advantage of milder temperatures and lighter snowfalls.

Marten young are born in litters of one to five. The *kits* reach adult size and have a full set of sharp teeth by 4 months. Young martens leave their mother by late summer or early autumn to search for a territory of their own.

The American pine marten (top) climbs trees to catch red squirrels, its most common prey. A single porcupine can provide two weeks of food for the fisher (below), a species of marten.

The barn owl (above) is recognized by its white heart-shaped face. It is commonly associated with farmlands, but can be found almost anywhere between latitudes 40°N to 40°S in habitats ranging from woodlands to towns.

Bird's-Eye View of the Forest

From perches high above the ground, predatory birds scan the forest and listen for sounds that mean food. Eggs and nest fledglings may attract hawks, magpies, and owls. For owls, nibbling noises might mean that a mouse or a rabbit is hidden in the grass. For ravens or magpies, the howling of a wolf might lead to a fresh kill nearby.

Owls Owls are found in various habitats on every continent except Antarctica. The **eastern screech owl** and the **barn owl** are two of the species common to North and South America. Some 30 subspecies of barn owls are widely distributed in habitats across the Americas and Europe. Because they prey on mice and rats, barn owls are welcomed by farmers. One family of barn owls can eat up to 1,300 rodents a year.

All owls are carnivores, eating only live prey. Other distinguishing features include soft downy feathers, sharp beaks, and flat faces. Most owls have good night vision. Their huge pupils allow the retina, the light-sensitive layer at the back of the eye, to function in very low light. Owls' eyes are tubular rather than spherical and cannot move from side to side in their sockets. To make up for this characteristic, owls are able to turn their head more than a half circle in either direction.

Acute hearing also contributes to owls' success as night hunters. Their ears are so sensitive that they can detect the sound of a mouse's footsteps 30 feet (9 m) below on the forest floor.

Like all owls, great horned owls (left), may spend their entire lives in one territory. The great gray owl (above) often hunts during the day. Some great gray owls have tails as long as 12 inches (31 cm) long.

The circle of stiff feathers around each ear acts like a satellite dish, capturing sound waves and channeling them to the ear. In addition, many species of owls have a tuft of feathers on either side of their head that looks like an ear but is not. They use these feathers as part of their threat display, spreading their wings and fluffing up their feathers to twice their normal size. The soft, downy feathers in their wings also help to muffle the sound of their beating wings as they swoop toward prey.

Owls prey on many of the animals in their environment, including rabbits, rats, muskrats, woodcocks, and grouse. Many owls also eat fish, insects, frogs, and snakes. Most swallow their prey whole and later regurgitate a pellet containing indigestible elements such as fur, bones, and feathers.

An owl found in coniferous forests worldwide is the **great gray owl. Horned owls** and **long-eared owls** are also associated with northern forests. The powerful **great horned owl** lives in the Americas in habitats that include swamps, prairies, deserts, and forests. Female great horned owls are larger than males. Great horned owls have brown-and-white speckled plumage and a wingspan up to 4.5 feet (1.4 m). Their legs are feathered down to the feet, offering protection against struggling prey. In the last second of their swift, silent descent, the owls swing their feet forward to catch prey in their talons. Then their sharp, hooked bill tears the prey apart.

Zoo Medicine

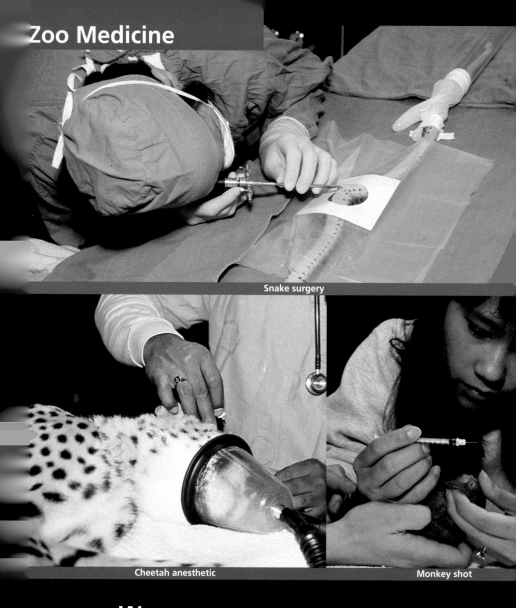

Snake surgery

Cheetah anesthetic

Monkey shot

What happens when animals at the zoo get sick? Most zoos have permanent medical teams that provide routine and emergency care. A team usually consists of a veterinarian, a laboratory technician, and a pathologist, who studies and diagnoses diseases.

The medical team's responsibilities are as varied as the animals they take care of. A typical day's work may include giving a elephant to see if she is pregnant, and quarantining a rhinoceros that has just arrived from another zoo.

Sick baby animals are carefully monitored by zoo staff. Recovered infants are reunited with their parents. Rearing by humans is usually avoided.

Zoo veterinarians perform surgery as well. In 1994, the first open-heart surgery on an orangutan was performed at the San

Gorilla dental checkup

Tiger blood pressure

Elephant ultrasound

Carrying out these duties is challenging for zoo personnel. Certain animals can be persuaded to remain still while being examined. Some elephants will allow blood samples to be taken from a vein behind the ear. Other animals, including chimpanzees, have proven to be willing patients if a food reward is provided.

Most animals, however, must be sedated before the medical team can examine and treat them. Using tranquilizers on zoo animals was once a very dangerous practice. Animals sometimes died if they were given dosages higher than their bodies could handle; or caretakers were injured by animals who were not given a high enough dosage to put them to sleep.

Today, experienced zoo medicine teams can rely upon advanced research and sophisticated techniques that enable them to give zoo animals the best possible medical attention.

Animals of the Mountains

From the Andes of Ecuador to the Himalayas of Tibet, the mountains of the world represent a diverse biome. Only animals such as llamas, yaks, and mountain goats, specifically adapted to mountainous terrain and altitude, are found at high elevations. On the lower slopes live many animals that are equally at home in other environments.

An American bighorn ram stands in the grass at Northwest Trek Wildlife Park in Washington state.

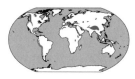

One Biome, Many Habitats

Mountain habitats differ according to their altitude and latitude. As altitude increases, climate and animal and plant life gradually change. Both temperate and tropical mountains are generally cooler and wetter at high elevations. Near the summit, tropical mountains often are enveloped in clouds. There, trees are shorter and covered with mosses. In temperate mountains, the coniferous forest ends in a zone of stunted trees, above which lies the timberline, where tree growth stops because of poor soil, cold temperatures, drying winds, and ice cover.

The timberline does not mean the end of all vegetation, however. Low grasses and ground-hugging plants grow in alpine meadows above timberline, and higher still, lichens and mosses provide food for hardy grazing animals. Because the highest slopes are often harsh and bare, the number of animal species decreases as altitude increases. Animals often migrate up and down mountains, according to weather conditions or the vegetation in season at a particular altitude.

Wildflowers and fir trees at the base of Mount Rainier in Washington state show the diversity of vegetation that grows in mountain regions.

On the Brink of Extinction

Giant pandas, spectacled bears, and snow leopards live in some of the most remote and mountainous regions of the world. Each of these species is close to extinction. In recent years their ranges have been shrinking under pressure from hunters and human expansion.

Giant Panda Today the giant panda is protected in China, where approximately 1,000 are left in the wild, living in mountains at the eastern rim of the Tibetan plateau. Recent studies based on molecular techniques place this panda in the bear family, while the much smaller **red panda**, a separate species, is a member of the raccoon family. Giant pandas weigh between 165 and 242 pounds (75–110 kg). Male pandas tend to be larger than females, although both look similar.

Pandas live in areas where bamboo grows abundantly, between altitudes of 6,000 and 11,000 feet (2,000–3,500 m). Large molars enable them to chew tough bamboo stalks. Because bamboo is not very nutritious, and because they have less efficient digestive systems than most herbivores, pandas must eat approximately 33 pounds (15 kg) of bamboo stems and leaves each day to extract sufficient nutrients. Pandas occasionally supplement their diet with grass, bulbs, fish, and small rodents. Pandas eat sitting up, holding a bamboo stem in flexible paws. They strip off the outer sheath of the bamboo with their thumb, which is actually an enlarged wristbone.

There is currently only one giant panda in North America, located at the National Zoo in Washington, D.C. At the same zoo, a female panda, then the oldest outside China, died in 1992. Because pandas are extremely difficult to breed in zoos, preservation efforts focus on protecting pandas in their natural habitat. In the wild, females give birth in late summer to cubs weighing only 3 to 5 ounces (85–150 g), making the mother 900 times the weight of her offspring.

What to look for

Pandas are shortsighted, an indication of their solitary lives in the wild.

They communicate by vocalizations and by posture. Putting the head between the front legs signals submission. Lowering the head and staring signals aggression.

Pandas groom by rubbing the head and face with their front paws.

Breeding pandas in zoos is difficult and often unsuccessful. Artificial insemination has also produced mixed results.

What to look for

Spectacled bears are named for the conspicuous white circles of fur around their eyes.

They also have whitish markings on their head and chest.

They have relatively small heads and snouts.

Spectacled Bear The spectacled bear, a shaggy black animal named for the tawny white circles on its face, lives in South America, where it is the only bear species. Found primarily in tropical mountains, it also inhabits grasslands and semideserts. It stands 30 inches (75 cm) high and weighs up to 308 pounds (140 kg). Its hooklike claws make it the best tree climber in the bear family.

Avid fruit eaters, spectacled bears sometimes assemble a platform of broken branches in a fruit tree, on which they feed and nap. Primarily herbivorous, they also occasionally eat rodents and insects. If near human habitation, they feed on crops such as sugar cane and corn. They do not hibernate.

After spectacled bears mate, they stay together for less than two weeks. Between the ages of three and eight months, the cubs begin to hunt with the mother. Like other bear cubs, the young give a high-pitched distress call when alarmed.

Spectacled bears are usually solitary but occasionally form small family groups. They live in the Andes Mountains at heights of up to 10,000 feet (3,000 m).

Snow Leopard The snow leopard of Central Asia, a ghostly gray cat with black spots, black circles, and a creamy-white belly, is seldom seen. It weighs up to about 155 pounds (70 kg). One of the most agile of the big cats, it can jump from a rocky crag 60 feet (20 m) high, the equivalent of leaping to the ground from the top of a six-story building.

Snow leopards rarely travel below 9,800 feet (3,000 m). In summer they move to the cooler air of higher elevations, as high as 18,000 feet (5,500 m), where they often bathe in mountain streams and pools. They hunt wild goats and sheep, such as the bharal, or blue sheep, of Nepal, which live on the sparse vegetation of alpine pastures. Because prey is scarce at high altitudes, snow leopards range over large territories and will take any prey, from a 600-pound (275 kg) yak to a 6-pound (3 kg) rodent. They seldom leave a kill until they have eaten everything but the skeleton and hide.

Like other leopards, snow leopards are solitary except during the mating season. The two or three cubs in a litter travel with the mother at three months, staying with her through their first winter. In zoos, snow leopards have lived up to 19 years.

Snow leopards are threatened by hunters, who sell their pelts on the black market. Other hunters kill the mountain sheep that are the leopards' major food. An estimated 3,000 snow leopards remain in the wild.

The snow leopard can spring onto prey from up to 50 feet (15 m) away. Although it is one of the big cats, the snow leopard eats in a crouched position as do small cats. It also does not roar like other big cats.

Hooves

Zebra

Rhinoceros

Animals with hooves are known as ungulates. Most ungulates are fast runners and sure-footed. They are usually divided into two groups, depending on the number of toes they have.

Odd-toed ungulates include horses, zebras, tapir, and rhinos. Odd-toed animals have either one toe or three weight-bearing toes on each foot. In horses and zebras, the hoof is the third toe of each

What to look for

Yaks have curved horns, which grow from the sides of the head.

They have long fringes of silky hair on their chests, tails, and flanks.

Female yaks and their calves live in small herds of ten to twelve animals. Despite their size, yaks are agile and can climb down steep inclines or swim across rivers.

Sure-Footed Travelers

Yaks Related to wild cattle, two species of yak live in the high mountains and plateaus of central Asia and are adapted to altitudes of up to 20,000 feet (6,000 m). **Wild yaks** weigh as much as 2,200 pounds (1,000 kg) and are over 6 feet (2 m) tall at the shoulder. They have adapted to the sparse diet of the Tibetan plateau, and maintain their massive bulk by grazing on grasses, herbs, and lichens. Yaks have an abundance of oxygen-absorbing red blood cells to make efficient use of the thin air at high altitudes.

Today only a few hundred wild yaks remain of the thousands that once roamed the high Tibetan plateau. However, the smaller **domestic yak** totals around 12 million in Central Asia. Yaks walk slowly but tirelessly; domestic yaks can carry 300-pound (150 kg) loads over high mountain passes.

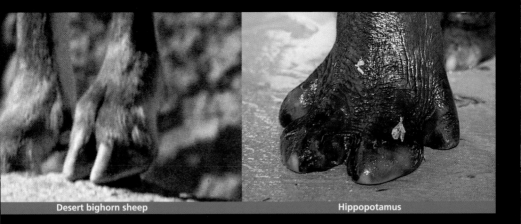

Desert bighorn sheep

Hippopotamus

foot, the others having disappeared during evolution. Tapir are the only odd-toed mammals native to the Americas. Rhinos are the largest of the odd-toed mammals, having three toes on each foot.

Even-toed ungulates such as hippos, antelope, mountain goats, and bison have two or four weight-bearing toes on each foot. Two toes can spread apart to provide traction in rough terrain.

Llama The llama is a domesticated animal adapted for life in the mountains. A single species is found in the Andes from southern Peru to northwestern Argentina. A member of the camel family, the llama has a long dense coat in shades of brown, black, or white. Zoologists believe the llama is descended from the **guanaco**, another member of the camel family that still lives in the wild in South America.

Llamas can carry loads of 100 pounds (45 kg) or more for up to 20 miles (30 km). They eat scrubby bushes and coarse mountain grass. About three million llamas are used as pack animals today, though as a means of transport they are slowly being replaced by trucks and trains.

Vicuña The llama's relative in the wild, the vicuña, is also found in the Andes in semiarid grasslands and plains at elevations of 12,000 to 15,700 feet (3,500–5,000 m). Swift and agile, it can run up to 30 miles per hour (50 km/h). It is the only hoofed animal with continuously growing teeth—a trait more common to rodents—which are useful for close cropping of tough mountain plants. The vicuña's wool is used by humans to make camel hair coats.

When threatened, the llama (top) spits foul-smelling saliva. The vicuña (above) has separate feeding and sleeping territories.

Mountain Goat The shaggy, pure-white mountain goat is found in western North America. Both males and females grow small curved black horns. Weighing up to 310 pounds (140 kg), mountain goats scramble up cliff faces that offer only tiny footholds. Expert scalers, they can climb up 1,500 feet (450 m) of steep terrain in 20 minutes without strain. Mountain goats eat grasses, shrubs, lichens, and mosses year-round, uncovering the plants from the snow when necessary.

In winter, mountain goats migrate to lower altitudes, where they still endure gale-force winds, deep snowdrifts, and temperatures as low as −50° F (−45° C). They are protected by a winter coat

The age of a mountain goat can be determined by the number of rings on its horns. The first ring develops at two years of age. Mountain goats develop an additional ring each spring.

8 inches (20 cm) long and by dense underfur as fine as cashmere. Although they shed their winter coat in the spring, mountain goats spend much of the summer trying to stay cool. By lying on banks of melting snow and keeping to shaded slopes they also reduce assaults by biting insects.

The Mountain Goat

Short sharp horns for defense

Thick woolly coat adapted to snowy conditions

Beard signifies a male

Small cushioned hooves for moving on rocky cliffs

Short sturdy legs for balance on steep terrain

Mountain goats do not huddle like sheep. They prefer to stay up to 8 feet (2.5 m) apart from one another, and will vigorously defend their space. When threatened by another goat, a mountain goat may stare at its opponent, or turn sideways and arch its back, thereby increasing its apparent size. As a last resort, it may charge.

After mating in fall or early winter, females give birth to one kid, or occasionally two, in late May or early June. Kids begin to practice climbing and leaping during the first day of life. They lift up their tail when they want the mother's milk or her attention. Adult mountain goats make the same gesture when they are frightened.

American mountain bighorn sheep migrate to lower elevations when food becomes scarce, thereby avoiding competition for food with mountain goats.

Mountain Bighorn Sheep Sometimes known as American bighorn sheep, mountain sheep live in the same high regions as mountain goats. The largest of the mountain sheep is found in the Pamir Mountains of the Himalayas. Bighorn sheep of North America can weigh up to 300 pounds (140 kg). In contrast to goats, which have sharp horns and fragile skulls, mountain sheep have rounded horns and massive skulls and can butt one another without doing severe damage. Unlike desert bighorn sheep (see p. 117), mountain sheep live in large flocks; the males often engage in prolonged duels to establish leadership.

Mountain sheep live in open lands near cliffs; mountain goats live on cliffs, where predators cannot easily pursue them.

The **Barbary sheep,** of a different genus from the mountain bighorn sheep, is a common sheep in zoos. It inhabits the mountains of North Africa, where its light-brown coat provides excellent camouflage in a rocky habitat.

Hunting in Varied Terrain

Red Fox A member of the dog family, the red fox is one of the most widely dispersed foxes in the world. It is found in a variety of habitats, including mountains, in Eurasia and North America. It is also found in Australia, where it was introduced in the nineteenth century. Red foxes range in color from pale red to brown. The so-called **silver fox** is actually a red fox with a recessive gene. Red foxes vary in size, some adults weighing only 7 pounds (3 kg), and others, in northern latitudes, as much as 30 pounds (14 kg).

Red foxes have tremendous endurance. If chased, they can run at 30 miles per hour (50 km) for several miles, leaping obstacles 6 feet (2 m) high and swimming across rivers and streams. Primarily nocturnal, they have excellent night vision.

Red foxes are excellent hunters. If their prey escapes, they may curl up for a nap near its burrow, waiting for its reappearance. Their sensitive ears can identify the rustling of small animals under two feet (60 cm) of snow. In addition to rodents, foxes eat hares, birds, snakes, frogs, insects, fruit, and berries.

Able to eat only about a pound of meat at a time, red foxes often bury, or *cache,* abundant prey in summer and dig it up later when food is scarce. Fox cubs, called kits, imitate the cache ritual with bits of meat they find around the den.

The red fox (below and bottom) sleeps in the open except when raising young in a den. Red foxes communicate with howls, barks, whimpers, and yaps.

Weasels Weasels and polecats are widely distributed in a variety of habitats across Eurasia, North Africa, and the Americas. Their skull and body are thin, their legs short, and their flexible spine allows them to maneuver in the narrow tunnels of their prey. The **common weasel** and the **least weasel** are smaller than most weasels, weighing only up to 7 ounces (200 g).

Furred pads on their feet help weasels to run quickly over snow. Like most small mammals, they have a high metabolic rate and a ravenous appetite. Weasels consume their weight in food every day and must eat five to ten times daily. Primarily carnivores, weasels prey upon mice, rabbits, voles (small, mouselike rodents), birds, and birds' eggs. A weasel can run while carrying a hare more than twice its weight. In relation to their size, weasels are stronger than lions, which cannot run carrying prey even half their weight.

One of the most common species in the weasel family is the **ermine**, or stoat, which is found in the mountains and lowlands of North America and Eurasia. Larger than the common weasel, the ermine is dark brown with white underparts in summer, and white with a black-tipped tail in winter. Its winter coat provides useful camouflage in the snow, concealing it from predators such as hawks, owls, and foxes. Like other weasels, ermines build dens in rocky crevices, hollow logs, or abandoned rodent burrows, or among tree roots.

Using its flexible backbone, an ermine (left) sits up on its hind legs to get a better view of its surroundings. The Kolinsky, or Siberian, weasel (right) has a dark brown coat that turns paler, but not white, in winter.

Otters Found on every continent except Australia and Antarctica, otters are more at home in the water than any other members of the weasel family. Some otters, such as the **Sumatran otter** of Southeast Asia, live near mountain rivers and streams, but most otters are found in lowland lakes, rivers and coastal waters. The **American river otter,** which is distributed across North America, weighs up to 25 pounds (11 kg). The **European river otter** is about the same size and is also widely dispersed. Destruction of habitat threatens the survival of most otter species.

Otters can move almost as fast on land as in the water. Preying mostly on fish and waterfowl, they sometimes catch fish by chasing them into shallow inlets. Both American and European river otters have between one and five young in each litter. Otters in zoos often chase one another and seem playful.

What to look for

Otters' webbed feet are useful in their largely aquatic environment.

Their long, flattened, tapered tails help them steer while swimming.

Most otters have claws; their back feet are longer than their front feet.

Night Vision

Like most carnivores, weasels have a reflective layer of tissue, called a *tapetum lucidum,* behind the retina of their eyes to improve their night vision. Like a mirror, this tissue reflects any light that enters, increasing the light's strength. The reflected light makes the eyes of many predators seem to glow in the dark. The eyes of a weasel caught directly in the beam of a flashlight are a vivid green.

Stiff whiskers on the American river otter's snout help it to sense underwater movement and to track down prey.

187

Because the mink cannot see well underwater, it must watch for fish from land and then dive into the water to catch them.

Badgers Also members of the weasel family, badgers live in large, deep burrows in mountains and lowlands. They use their wide, flat body to block their den entrance, and their powerful claws to fight off attackers. They have long snouts and a well-developed sense of smell. Badgers hunt by digging up the underground dens of their prey.

The **Eurasian badger** is common in woodlands throughout Eurasia and weighs 22 to 44 pounds (10–20 kg). Its diet includes small mammals, insects, beetles, snails, worms, roots, fruits, and acorns. The smaller **North American badger,** of a different genus than Eurasian badgers, weighs up to 26 pounds (12 kg) and eats carrion and invertebrates in addition to small mammals. Its predators include coyotes and eagles. A strong swimmer, it hunts both night and day.

Mink The **American mink** is almost as dependent on access to water as the river otter. It has a narrow territory not more than 150 to 300 ft (50–100 m) from a lake or riverbank, where it preys on fish, small mammals, and birds, storing its catch and feeding on it later. Both the American mink and the less common **European mink** were once hunted for their pelts. The decline of the fur trade has made mink less threatened, though they are still often destroyed as pests because they attack domestic stock such as chickens.

Although the North American badger sometimes mates in the fall, its fertilized eggs do not begin to develop until after the winter. This adaptation ensures that the young will be born when food is more plentiful.

In the spring, the hoary marmot (left) comes out of hibernation to clean out its burrow. Pikas (above right) spend nearly half of their time perched on rocks within their territory. From there they call, in short squeaks, to attract mates.

Burrowers in the Mountains

Pikas Small, round mammals about the size of a guinea pig, pikas live in the mountains of North America and Eurasia at altitudes of up to 20,000 feet (6,000 m). They are among the many burrowing animals preyed on by foxes and weasels. In the Rocky Mountains, pikas bark to warn of hawks or coyotes.

Marmots Marmots, relatives of the prairie dog and members of the large squirrel family of rodents, are also burrowers in the mountainsides of Eurasia and North America. The **hoary marmot** is a bushy-tailed resident of northern Canada and Alaska; the **alpine marmot** ranges from central Europe to Siberia. Marmots form colonies in open meadows, where they dig burrows up to 20-feet (6 m) deep and tunnels up to 200-feet (60 m) long. Unlike pikas, marmots hibernate in winter, sometimes for as long as nine months. They prepare for their long sleep by gorging on a diet of grasses and other green vegetation, increasing their body fat by about 20 percent.

The most familiar species of marmot in the United States is the **woodchuck,** known also as the **groundhog,** common to both mountains and valley farmlands. Unlike other marmots, woodchucks live in separate burrows and do not form large colonies.

Bald eagles (above left and right) often chase ospreys or gulls and take their prey. The peregrine falcon (below) has been used for centuries for hunting in many parts of the world. Female peregrines are slightly larger than males.

Birds of the Mountains

Mountain birds include bald eagles, golden eagles, hawks, falcons, jays, partridge, quail, grouse, and ravens. All of these birds are also found in various habitats at lower elevations.

Eagles The **golden eagle** (see p. 94) and the **bald eagle** are birds of prey, also known as *raptors*. The national bird of the United States, the adult bald eagle is easily recognized by its snowy white head, neck, tail, and rump. It is approximately 30 inches (75 cm) long, with a wingspread of about 7.5 feet (2.5 m). Like many other birds of prey, female bald eagles are larger than males. Bald eagles eat primarily fish, as well as seabirds and carrion. They nest in trees near oceans and mountain lakes.

Habitat destruction and pesticides are a major threat to the survival of the bald eagle. As certain pesticides have been banned, the bald eagle population has slowly increased. In 1994 there were an estimated 4,000 breeding pairs of bald eagles in the lower United States.

Falcons Smaller than eagles, falcons are also birds of prey. The size of a large crow, the **peregrine falcon** frequents many habitats in all continents except Antarctica. A swift flyer, it preys on small birds, which it strikes in the air with its feet. Less swift than the peregrine is the **brown falcon**, which inhabits New Guinea and Australia.

Ravens Often confused with crows because of their jet black feathers, ravens are larger and more powerful, with a wingspan of 4 feet (1.25 m). Male ravens dive and tumble in the air to win the attention of females, in a ritual that, if successful, ends with two ravens mating for life. Ravens have a number of calls, the most common being a deep, resonant *quork quork*.

The California Condor

Fossil records indicate that the California condor once ranged from western Canada to Mexico and east to Florida By the 1940s, however, its range was limited to a small mountainous area of California. As fruit and vegetable farms replaced cattle and sheep ranches, the condors lost their major source of food—dead livestock. Poisoned carrion, pesticides, and electrocution from power lines also contributed to the condor's decline and its placement on the endangered species list.

In 1986, the San Diego Wild Animal Park and the Los Angeles Zoo were given permission by federal courts to bring surviving wild condors into a recovery program. The goal was to restore the condor population through careful breeding Once their numbers had increased, the condors would be returned to the wild.

California condors lay only one egg at a time. However, if the egg is taken, the condor will lay another to replace it. Zoos can increase the number of eggs that a female produces by removing eggs from the nest so that more eggs will be produced The removed eggs hatch in incubators. To prevent incubated condor chicks from imprinting (see pp. 96–97) on human zookeepers, condor puppets are used to feed them.

Controlled breeding has increased the condor population from 15 birds in 1985 to 89 in 1994. Even more promising is the fact that several California condors have been released and now live in the Southern California Sespe Condor Sanctuary.

In flight, the California condor is a truly impressive sight. With a wingspan of nearly 10 feet (3 m), it is big enough to be mistaken at a distance for an airplane. The California condor is also one of the heaviest flying birds, weighing up to 25 pounds (11 kg). It is covered with black feathers, except for its head, neck, and feet, which are bare pink skin.

Animals of the Ice and Tundra

The most remote outposts of animal life on Earth lie within the Arctic and Antarctic Circles. Many animals of these regions, including penguins and polar bears, are large and have thick coats and layers of insulating fat. However, not all polar animals live in entirely frozen habitats. Climates and landscapes differ by latitude and range from vistas of ice to open fields of moss and grass.

Naturalistic zoo exhibits strive to re-create the environment of antarctic animals such as these Adélie penguins.

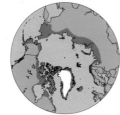

Polar Geography

The lands nearest the North Pole (right), and the South Pole (left), are covered with frozen ice and snow, shown in white. Bordering these areas is a region of tundra, shown in dark brown, where summers are warm enough to allow some vegetation to grow.

Polar bears (top) are usually solitary, to avoid competing with other bears for food. Musk oxen (above) live in herds and huddle for warmth and protection.

Adapting to a Harsh Environment

The Arctic is the youngest of the current world's ecosystems. Animal and plant life has been possible in the arctic only since the glaciers of the ice age retreated about 10,000 years ago. Considerable marine life thrives in the ocean under the floating ice of the Arctic. The ice at the North Pole is at most 7 feet (21.5 m) thick, but it creates the illusion of land. The floating ice cap extends southward until it overlaps land in the northern reaches of Alaska, Canada, and Greenland. There, permanent ice cover gives way to tundra, a region of low trees and shrubs that is covered by snow for most of the year.

The short arctic summer frees most of the tundra region, except Greenland, of ice and snow. Then, flowers bloom and insects breed, attracting birds such as Lapland longspurs and snow buntings from the south that migrate north to nest. Even in summer, the frozen earth, or permafrost, a few inches below the surface, never softens, and few species have time to adapt to the harsh environment.

Those animals that have adapted to the Arctic are highly interdependent. Polar bears normally eat only the blubber and internal organs of the seals they kill. The rest of the carcass

serves as food for foxes and seabirds. By pawing away snow from tundra vegetation for their own consumption, musk oxen expose food for arctic hares and ptarmigan.

Antarctica As harsh as the arctic environment is, it seems mild compared to that of the continent of Antarctica. The land mass at the South Pole is covered by an ice cap more than a mile (1.6 km) thick, overlaid with as much as 300 feet (90 m) of snow. Winter temperatures may fall to −70°F (−57°C), and blizzards rage for days on end.

A gentoo penguin (right) discourages the chinstrap that strays into its path. Chinstraps are exclusive to the Antarctic, whereas gentoos are also found in the more temperate Falkland Islands.

There is no permanent human population on Antarctica, although scientists from many countries conduct research there. No land mammals live in Antarctica. Yet, because of upwellings of nutrient-rich waters from ocean currents, the ocean around the continent abounds in fish and other marine life. These waters provide food for marine mammals, such as seals and whales. Seabirds crowd Antarctica's coastal cliffs and ledges, areas that are relatively free of snow.

Scientists at more than 30 bases on Antarctica conduct research in such fields as animal behavior, environmental studies, geology, oceanography, and meteorology.

Giants of the North

Large mammals conserve heat more effectively than small ones, making size an advantage in the Arctic. Two giants of the north, polar bears and musk oxen, illustrate successful adaptation to the harsh conditions there.

Polar Bear A close relative of the brown bear, the polar bear is now classified as a separate genus. Yet polar bears can hybridize with brown bear in zoos, and the female hybrids are fertile.

Found on ice floes and near coastal waters in the far northern regions of the world, polar bears are protected from the cold by a layer of fat 2 to 4 inches (5–10 cm) thick. In the coldest weather they curl up like sled dogs, with their backs against the wind, or burrow in the snow. Adult polar bears weigh an average of 800 pounds (363 kg). In summer, melting pack ice forces polar bears to come ashore in the more southerly parts of their range. There they forage on birds, rodents, and carrion, but unlike most mammals, they actually lose weight in summer.

Patient hunters, polar bears often wait for hours near breathing holes where ringed seals surface. They also stalk seals that bask on the ice. Their noses are sensitive enough to sniff seal dens covered by 3 feet (1 m) of ice and snow. Their broad, wide feet, measuring up to 12 inches (30 cm) long, provide traction as they walk on thin ice.

The polar bear cub (top) remains with its mother for two to five years. To protect their cubs, females avoid other polar bears, especially males, who may kill the young.

The Polar Bear

Small ears help conserve heat.

Thick water-repellent fur and fat layer conserve heat.

Keen sense of smell enhances hunting skills.

Sharp claws ensure traction on ice while sealhunting.

Fur-covered feet are partially webbed for swimming.

Polar bears rely on a diet of meat more than other bears. Their sharp molars are adapted for shearing through flesh, and their curved, needle-sharp claws allow them to grasp struggling prey. Their digestive tract contains enzymes and bacteria that are especially adapted for digesting meat, and their stomach can hold about 150 pounds (70 kg) of food.

Polar bears are the most aquatic of all bears, sometimes diving to the ocean floor for mussels and kelp. When they plunge into water, their ears flatten, their nostrils close, and thin transparent eyelids cover their eyeballs. They use their back feet for steering and their front feet for locomotion, like flippers. They have been found swimming 20 miles (30 km) or more offshore.

In October or November, pregnant polar bears dig a den in a snowbank. The den consists of a tunnel leading to one or more oval chambers about 9 feet (3 m) in diameter. The packed snow traps the mother's heat and provides effective insulation in the middle of the arctic winter. The cubs are born about nine months later. When they emerge from the den, about three months after birth, they follow their mother everywhere, and even ride on her back when she swims.

Musk oxen With their humped shoulders and shaggy coats, musk oxen resemble a distant relative, the American bison. Some musk oxen weigh as much as 650 pounds (295 kg). Their dense, woolly underfur is eight times warmer than sheep's wool. Combined with thick layers of fat, this underfur helps them maintain a constant body temperature of around 101°F (38° C) even in weather of −40°F (−40°C). In spring and summer they shed the underfur in long, untidy strips. Musk oxen become overheated easily in warm weather and sometimes get necessary water by eating mouthfuls of snow.

During the mating season, male musk oxen emit a musky scent from a gland located below their eyes. Because they feed on plants beneath the snow, musk oxen live only in areas where the snow cover is thin.

Musk oxen live in herds of 10 or fewer in summer, and in larger herds of as many as 100 in winter. The herds wander, grazing on grasses and rushlike plants called sedges during the short growing season and browsing on twigs from plants such as evergreen and willow shrubs in winter. Agile and sure-footed, they have sharp-edged, concave hooves that have become adapted for traction on rocky ground and icy terrain.

During the summer rut, males fight for possession of females, charging from 20 to 30 feet (6–9 m) apart and crashing their horns and thick skulls together. When threatened, musk ox males encircle the females and calves. Though an effective defense against wolves, this tactic is tragically unsuccessful against human hunters, who easily corner the herd and shoot its largest members.

What to look for

Both male and female musk oxen have horns that grow hard and flat over the skull, curving outward from the sides of the head.

Musk oxen's long, coarse, dark brown guard hair grows up to 2 feet (60 cm) long.

Survival in a Frozen Land

Hares that live on the tundra are good examples of the adaptation of smaller animals to arctic conditions. They browse on grasses during summer and dig under the snow for willow, birch, and heather in winter. Arctic foxes are also at home on ice and tundra, having found a niche as both scavengers and hunters. They follow polar bears over the ice to eat the leftovers of seals they kill, and prey on lemmings, hares, and ground-nesting birds on the tundra.

Arctic hare The arctic hare is found in Alaska, Canada, Scandinavia, and Siberia, living in burrows on the tundra. Pockets of arctic hares are also found farther south, in Ireland and the Alps, for example. Like all hares, arctic hares have dense fur on the soles of their feet, but they are larger and rounder than most other hare species. Their short ears, compared with the longer ears of their relatives in temperate regions, conserve heat efficiently.

In their most northerly ranges arctic hares are white year-round, whereas those farther south shed their brown summer coat for a white one in winter. Irish hares retain their reddish-brown coat all year. Less prolific than other hares, arctic hares have one litter of two to five young in spring or summer.

Arctic hares grow to at least 2 feet (60 cm) in length and may weigh as much as 12 pounds (5 kg). Sometimes found in small groups, they are usually solitary animals.

What to look for

Arctic foxes have relatively short legs and fur-covered soles.

Their fur is white, except for a black-tufted tail in winter; in summer their fur has creamier tones. Some foxes' coats turn shades of blue gray.

The arctic fox feeds at the seashore at low tide, when snails and other marine creatures are fresh and plentiful.

Arctic Fox The arctic fox, also known as the blue fox, has a dense, woolly coat. Compared with foxes in temperate zones, it has a plumper body, shorter tail, and rounder face. These adaptations conserve heat and prevent frostbite.

Primarily nocturnal, arctic foxes travel long distances across the ice and tundra, eating any food, dead or alive, that they can find. In a study of this species, a journey of 930 miles (1,500 km) in a single year was recorded for one fox. Aggressive hunters, hungry arctic foxes will snatch scraps from polar bears and wolves. They often squabble among themselves over food. If caught in a blizzard, they burrow into a snowdrift for shelter.

Arctic foxes dig permanent dens in the tundra but stay near the den only when raising young. Some dens are used for centuries and gradually acquire dozens of entrances. Arctic foxes mate for life and usually raise one litter of six to twelve kits each year. Like arctic hares, the kits develop quickly and become independent when scarcely more than a month old.

Creating a
Polar Environment

Building a polar environment at the zoo involves a creative cast of designers, architects, curators, and scientists. Their goal is to re-create a natural setting that will encourage animals to behave as they do in the wild.

Polar bears, walruses, penguins and seals have different needs; the exhibit design team must account for every feature of each animal's natural habitat.

For example, when designing an antarctic home for penguins, the physical environment must facilitate breeding, social interaction, and exercise. In addition, temperature is very important.

Refrigeration engineers install elaborate systems to control climate. The rocky coast of Antarctica is simulated by molded concrete. Real ice is created by streaming water across the cold, hard surface of the arti-

The number of penguins in a colony dictates the size of an exhibit. Curators and naturalists calculate the required number of square feet per penguin based on observations of penguins in the wild.

Ledges and crevices for nesting are built in, and pebbles are scattered around the exhibit area. Penguins use pebbles to build their nests. To the human eye all the pebbles may look the same, but penguins squawk and fight over special pebbles.

Penguins depend on photoperiodism, or different periods of light and darkness, to tell them when to mate. Daylight hours are adjusted to stimulate breeding.

Penguins love diving into cold water, swimming, and shooting to the surface. Pools must be large, deep, and cold to encourage lots of aquatic exercise. Most zoos use fresh water instead of salt water be-

Double Lives on Ice and in the Sea

Among the most abundant animals in polar regions are walruses and seals, marine mammals that feed on the bounty of the sea. These creatures are well adapted for swimming and foraging in the ocean. They have limited mobility on land although they breed and give birth there.

Walrus A member of the seal family, the single species of walrus lives along the coasts of North Polar areas. Immense creatures, adult walruses weigh as much as 2,000 pounds (900 kg) and measure more than 11 feet (3.5 m) in length. Their tough, leathery hide is about an inch (2.5 cm) thick, and the layer of blubber beneath as much as 4 inches (10 cm) thick. Walruses can batter a hole through the thick arctic ice with their heavy, blunt heads. They lack external ears but have excellent hearing.

The walrus's lower snout has about 450 sensitive whiskers to help it locate food on the ocean floor. The upper snout has tough skin and is used for digging clams out of mud.

Both males and females have curved ivory tusks, which measure up to 3 feet (90 cm) in males. Tusks define rank in a herd, with the dominant male sporting the longest tusks. Walruses use their tusks like grappling hooks to haul themselves out of the water onto ice floes. They are also used as weapons in fights—both between males and females and between rival males during the mating season.

Walruses can dive to a depth of 300 feet (90 m), rooting on the sea floor for clams, mussels, and other mollusks. They use their back flippers to propel themselves through the water. Usually a bluish-white color when they surface, they dry to a russet brown after a few hours in the sun. Young walruses are darker in color than mature walruses.

During the winter breeding season, male walruses engage in repetitive calling, making bell-like or gong-like sounds, until they surface with shrill whistles. These sounds are thought to attract females and to deter competing males.

Walrus calves weigh 100 to 150 pounds (30–45 kg) at birth and are 3 to 4 feet (90–120 cm) long. They can survive immersion in cold seawater immediately after birth and can swim well in a week or two. Calves are nursed until about two years of age and are fiercely protected by the herd when threatened by predators. Orphaned calves are raised communally until they can fend for themselves.

Walruses (top) often huddle in herds of thousands on pack ice and rocky shores, resting their tusks on each other's backs. The walrus (above) uses its front flippers to support itself. Although clumsy on land, walruses are surprisingly agile in water (below).

Male elephant seals (above) have a greatly enlarged snout and weigh about three times as much as females. A few weeks after birth, a harp seal pup (right) will lose its white coat and develop a gray coat with brown spots.

Seals Many species of seals inhabit the oceans of both polar regions, where they feed on fish and crustaceans. In addition to walruses, there are two other seal families—eared seals and earless, sometimes called *true seals*. Although they have acute hearing, true seals lack external ears. The largest of all species of seals is the massive **elephant seal**, a true seal weighing between 4,500 and 9,000 pounds (2,000–4,000 kg). It is named for its long nose and trumpeting call. All seals mate and give birth on shore. During the breeding season, one male may protect 50 females in his breeding family.

The **leopard seal** is also a true seal and lives on the fringe of the Antarctic. Weighing up to 840 pounds (380 kg), it hunts underwater and often preys upon penguins.

A solitary animal, the leopard seal is the only seal that preys on other seals. It spends most of its time resting or hunting in the water near the edge of the ice.

The **arctic harp seal** is a smaller true seal, weighing about 390 pounds (175 kg). It is best known for the beautiful white fur of its pups, which is much sought after by fur traders. Because of international intervention, the hunting of harp seal pups is now strictly controlled.

This male northern fur seal is one of 14 species of eared seals. Unlike other seals, eared seals have external ear flaps. All seals have excellent hearing.

What to look for

Seals have thin, narrow nostrils, which they close when swimming underwater.

Their four legs have evolved into flippers for swimming.

Fur Seals Fur seals are eared seals and belong to the same seal family as sea lions. Unlike true seals, fur seals and sea lions use their front flippers for propulsion through water. The back flippers are adapted for traveling on land and for steering in water. Fur seals' coats have an inner layer of fine underfur and an outer layer of coarse, grayish brown guard hairs. Because their coat provides good insulation in the water, fur seals do not have as much fat as most other marine mammals.

Fur seals spend winter at sea but gather in the spring in breeding colonies, the females already pregnant from the previous year. Because only powerful males find mates, evolution has favored the development of larger and larger male fur seals, which often weigh three or four times as much as females.

Eight days after giving birth to a single pup, fur seal females breed again. The males fight each other for access to mates. The females must alternate between nursing their calf and foraging in the ocean for sealife to feed on. Fur seals often dive to depths of 125 feet (40 m), and sometimes as deep as 800 feet (250 m).

Nineteenth-century fur traders killed millions of fur seals for their pelts. In this century, however, protective measures have enabled these seals to make an extraordinary comeback. Today, the total population of fur seals in the wild is believed to be about two million.

The largest of all penguins, emperor penguins (above left and right) have one chick a year. Emperor penguin chicks are protected by their parents' bellies and supported by their feet.

Water Wings

In the Arctic and Antarctic the only reliable food supply lies underwater. Expert divers, seabirds in these regions feed on fish and other marine life, such as the tiny shrimplike crustaceans known as *krill*. Penguins do not fly at all, but instead swim after their food, using their wings as flippers to propel them through the water. Antarctic penguins can swim at speeds of 30 miles per hour (50 km/hr). Although they look similar to penguins, puffins, which belong to the auk family, use their short wings both to fly and to propel themselves through the water.

Penguins Most penguins live on remote or rocky shores in cold climates. Of the 17 species, only three, the **emperor penguin,** the **chinstrap penguin,** and the **Adélie penguin,** live on the Antarctic ice shelf. Other penguins are found in chilly coastal oceans off South America, Australia, New Zealand, and southern Africa. Even in the subtropics, penguins, such as the **Galápagos penguins** of the Galápagos Islands near the equator, are found in water chilled by ocean currents.

Penguins range in size from the tiny 12-inch (30-cm) **blue penguin** to the emperor penguin, more than 3 feet (1 m) long. Streamlined for diving and swimming, penguins have dense, waterproof feathers. They molt once a year and cannot swim until they have grown new feathers.

Penguins' feet are set far back on their body and are used as a rudder in the water. On land, this placement forces them to stand upright and waddle slowly. Fortunately, most penguins live in isolated areas where there are few land predators. Ocean predators include leopard seals and killer whales.

A penguin's bill has a razor-sharp cutting edge and a strong grip. The downward-curved bill of the emperor penguin allows it to catch fish efficiently. Other penguins may feed on squid or krill. Most can swim like porpoises, leaping above the surface of the water and opening their bills in the air to breathe.

Penguins lack binocular vision and judge distance by peering first with one eye and then with another, a practice that causes them to weave back and forth. Well insulated with fat, they often become overheated in warm weather. They respond by holding their flippers away from their bodies. Their flippers have a large surface area in relation to their bulk, and radiate heat effectively.

Most species of penguins breed on land or on ice floes in enormous colonies of as many as a million animals. With large numbers of penguins building nests and raising young, these colonies are noisy places of activity. Huddling in large groups reduces penguins' heat loss by 25 to 50 percent.

Male and female penguins of most species share the duties of incubation and feeding the young. Most penguins breed in spring and summer and make a nest of sticks and stones. Emperor penguins, however, breed in the fall. The male incubates a single egg by balancing it between his legs and on top of his feet under a protective flap of skin. He fasts for two months until relieved by the female.

Adélie penguins (above and below) display the black-and-white coloring characteristic of all penguins. Their black backs absorb sunlight to provide warmth. Their white bellies make it harder for predators to see them when swimming beneath them in the ocean.

What to look for

Most penguins have blue-gray or blue-black plumage and a white breast.

Male and female penguins look alike.

On land, penguins waddle in an upright position or toboggan on their belly, using their flippers to move along ice or snow.

Common puffins (left) shed the brightly colored sheath on their bill when breeding season ends. A tufted puffin (below) extends and flaps its wings before flying.

The female snowy owl is larger than the male. It has brown markings on its feathers. The male snowy owl is almost pure white. Both have feathers that cover and insulate their nostrils.

Common Puffin Of the three species of puffins, two are found in the North Pacific and the Bering Sea. The third species, the common puffin, or **Atlantic puffin,** lives in the North Atlantic. Common puffins are recognizable by their colorful triangular bill. Their body coloring, black above and white below, provides camouflage in water. The legs and feet are usually orange or bright red.

These rotund diving birds prey on fish, mollusks, and crustaceans in both coastal and offshore waters. They can carry up to ten small fish in their bill at a time. Common puffins form colonies of up to a million birds on cliffs or islands. Only during the breeding season, however, do puffins remain on land for extended periods of time.

To nest, a puffin uses its bill to dig a burrow measuring up to 4 feet (1.25 m) deep, often under a flat stone. Female puffins usually lay just one egg. Females do most of the incubating until the young are hatched, in about six weeks. Both male and female common puffins bring fish to their young for about 40 days. Most puffins do not breed until they are three years old.

Snowy Owl Unlike most owls, the handsome snowy owl is an active daytime hunter. Nesting in shallow hollows on arctic tundra, snowy owls prey on lemmings, hares, and seagulls. Larger than many other owl species, snowy owls average 23 inches (60 cm) in length. Sometimes forced to migrate in search of food, they have been seen as far south as Texas.

adaptation One or more traits of an organism that help it to survive and reproduce. The trait may be a pattern of behavior, such as seeking shelter from the sun's rays; a physiological process, such as reduced respiration during hibernation; or an anatomical feature, such as a prehensile tail for grasping branches.

alpine Relating to, inhabiting, or growing in mountainous regions above the timberline.

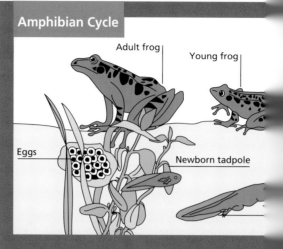

Amphibian Cycle

Adult frog | Young frog |

Eggs

Newborn tadpole

Free swimming amphibian larvae—tadpoles—live a fish-like existence in water. There they mature while breathing dissolved oxygen.

The tadpoles develop legs and simple lungs and lose their tails before emerging onto land—although some amphibians stay in water throughout

amphibian—marine toad

amphibian Any cold-blooded, vertebrate member of the class Amphibia, including frogs, toads, and salamanders. Most amphibians have characteristics that allow them to spend part of their life on land and part in the water. These include gills during the aquatic phase. All amphibians have moist skin, and many have webbed feet.

anticoagulant A substance that prevents blood from clotting. Vampire bats have an anticoagulant in their saliva to keep the blood of their prey flowing while they feed.

arid—Monument Valley

arid Very dry; lacking enough rainfall to support a wide variety of plant growth. A desert is arid land.

AZA American Zoo and Aquarium Association. Sometimes abbreviated *AZAA*.

big cat—Bengal tiger

big cat Any of the large members of the cat family belonging to the genus *Panthera*, including lions, tigers, leop-

Biome

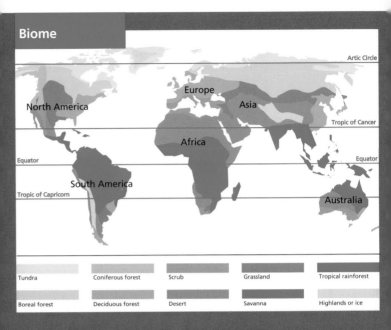

Tundra · **Coniferous forest** · **Scrub** · **Grassland** · **Tropical rainforest**

Boreal forest · **Deciduous forest** · **Desert** · **Savanna** · **Highlands or ice**

A community of animals and plants in a single, large ecological area. The boundaries of a biome are determined mostly by climate. The major biomes are tropical forests, grasslands, deserts, deciduous forests, coniferous forests, mountains, and permanent ice and tundra. A single biome may exist in many different areas of the world. For example, Africa, North and South America, and Asia all have grassland biomes.

ards, and jaguars. Compare **small cats.**

binocular vision Vision in which both eyes see an image simultaneously to produce a view in three dimensions. Primates have binocular vision.

biodiversity The overall biological distinctions of organisms and ecosystems within the biosphere.

biologist A scientist who specializes in biol-

ogy or in any of its subdisciplines.

biology The branch of science that deals with living organisms, including their life processes and ecology. Biology has many subdivisions.

biomass The total dry weight of the organisms in an ecosystem.

biopark A form of zoo that emphasizes the importance of nature as a whole, the interdependence of animal and

plant life, and the interactions between humanity and other life forms and nature.

biosphere All parts of Earth's crust, atmosphere, and waters that support life; also, the living organisms of the biosphere.

blubber A thick layer of fat lying under the skin and over the muscles of sea mammals such as walruses, whales, and seals. Blubber insulates against cold and is an energy source. It also helps streamline the animal for rapid movement through water.

boreal Relating to or characteristic of northern regions.

boreal forest Coniferous, evergreen forest adjacent to tundra in the northern, subarctic regions of North America, Europe, and Asia and marked by severe winters and short summers. Also called *taiga*.

brachiate To progress by means of brachiation.

brachiation Progression by means of swinging the arms and gripping one overhead hold after another. Gibbons and orangutans have specially adapted shoulder muscles to aid in brachiation from tree branch to tree branch.

brachiation

brachiator An animal that moves by brachiation.

bromeliad A tropical, chiefly epiphytic plant of the American pineapple family whose snug-fitting leaves are adapted to collect pools of water from which animals of the forest can drink.

browsing animal An animal that feeds chiefly on vegetation from trees and bushes. Rhinos and giraffes are browsing animals.

buck A male of various mammals, such as the deer, antelope, or rabbit.

bull An adult male of various mammals, such as elephant, elk, moose, bison, buffalo, or wildebeest.

buttress

buttress A thickened woody projection of the lower trunk of a tropical forest tree that helps keep the tree upright when the root system does not grow deep enough into the forest soil to provide a secure anchor. Buttresses mark a tree's maturity.

C

cache A secure hiding place for food, or the food hidden in such a

Bird of Prey

Bald eagle

A carnivorous bird that lives chiefly on the animals it captures in hunting. It will sometimes eat carrion. Powerful, swift fliers, birds of prey have excellent vision, powerful legs and feet, sharp talons, and a hooked beak. They typically seize their prey and fly off to devour it. Eagles, hawks, falcons, and owls are birds of prey.

Cell

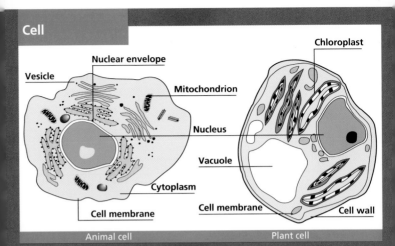

Animal cell

Plant cell

- Chloroplast
- Vesicle
- Nuclear envelope
- Mitochondrion
- Nucleus
- Vacuole
- Cytoplasm
- Cell membrane
- Cell membrane
- Cell wall

A cell is the smallest structural unit of living matter. It is usually microscopic in size and contains a nucleus.

Plants and animals are made up of many millions of cells, which perform specific functions within the organism. Types of cells

include muscle cells, nerve cells, and blood cells. Cells may be of various sizes and shapes, depending on their function.

place; also, to hide food in a cache. A red fox may cache some of its kill by burying it and covering the spot with leaves and twigs. A woodpecker preparing for winter may store acorns in caches it has bored in tree trunks.

camouflage A form of natural defense in which an organism's body colorings help it to blend in with its surroundings. The camouflage of the arctic hare is its white winter coat, which makes the hare hard to see in the snow.

canopy A forest's dense topmost layer,

formed by the branches, foliage, flowers, and fruit of forest trees and their associated vines.

captive breeding program Any program designed to increase the populations of endangered animals by breeding the animals in a zoo. Many animals bred in captive breeding programs are eventually released into the wild.

captivity The condition of an animal being kept in a zoo rather than living in the wild.

Carnivora An order of flesh-eating animals. Mammals that belong to

the order Carnivora include bears, cats, dogs, seals, and weasels.

carnivore Any animal of the order Carnivora.

carnivorous Feeding on flesh as the main source of food.

carrion Dead and decaying flesh of animals. Carrion is part of the diet of some mammals, such as hyenas, coyotes, opossums, and wolverines, and some birds, such as ravens and vultures.

cellulose A complex carbohydrate that is the main constituent of the cell walls of most plants.

clan A group of animals, such as hyenas or prairie dogs, living in close association.

class A major category of related animals or plants that ranks below a phylum and usually includes one or more orders.

cloud forest A tropical mountain forest lying at an altitude between 3,000 and 8,000 feet (914–2,438 m). Moist cloud forests have an abundance of epiphytes.

cold-blooded—iguana

cold-blooded Having no internal means of maintaining a more or less constant body temperature, and therefore relying on the external environment to control internal temperature. Fishes, reptiles, and amphibians are cold-blooded. *See* **warm-blooded.**

community The population of all the organisms that inhabit the same geographic area and interact with one another or are dependent on one another.

conifer Any of various mostly evergreen trees that bear cones and have needlelike leaves. Pine, spruce, and fir are conifers.

coniferous Relating to or being a conifer; having conifers as the predominant trees.

convergent evolution The evolution of similar structures or traits in organisms having separate lines of descent; for example, the skin-fold "wings" in flying squirrels and in flying opossums.

crustacean An invertebrate animal of the class Crustacea, including lobsters, crabs, and shrimps.

cud The food that a ruminant animal brings back up from its first stomach and chews again.

D

deciduous (Of tree or shrub) shedding or tending to shed the leaves annually in season, such as in autumn.

deforestation The process of clearing a forest by the large-scale cutting down and removal of its trees and other growth.

den The place of shelter of a wild animal, such as a fox.

doe The female of various mammals, such as the deer, antelope, or rabbit.

dormant Having biological activity suspended or greatly reduced, as an animal in hibernation.

E

echolocation *See* page 214.

ecological balance A state of equilibrium in which the ecological conditions and organisms of a region exist and interact in a mutually beneficial way. For example, the migration pattern of some grazing animals allows cropped grass to grow back.

ecology The scientific study of relationships

between living organisms and their living and nonliving surroundings; also, the set of relationships between organisms and their environment.

ecosystem A complex system formed by a community of organisms and the environment in which the community lives.

ectotherm A cold-blooded animal.

emergent A tall, isolated tree that rises above the rest of the canopy in a tropical for-

est and often serves as home and lookout post for birds of prey such as the monkey-eating eagle. An emergent may reach 200 feet (61 m) in height.

endangered species—
giant panda

endangered species A species that is in danger of becoming extinct, as through changes in climate or destruction of

its habitat. *See* **threatened species.**

endemic (Of a species) restricted to or found in only one geographic area.

environment The combination of all the elements in the surroundings of an organism or an ecological community—such as nutrients, temperature, air, soil, water, and other living things—that affect its form and survival.

epiphyte A plant that is not in contact with the ground and there-

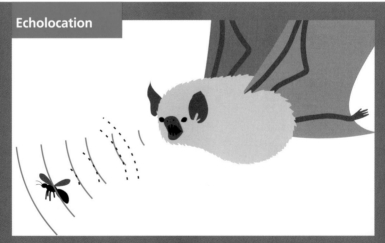

Echolocation

A system of locating objects by emitting high-pitched directional sounds that reflect off an object and return to the ears or other recep-

tors of the sender. Dolphins, whales and bats use echolocation to detect obstacles in dark surroundings or to locate prey.

Echolocating animals can determine the distance to, and the size and direction of, echo-reflecting objects much smaller than themselves.

Extinction

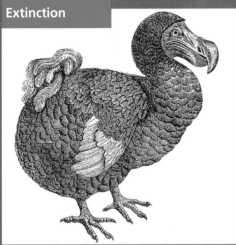

Dodo bird

The process by which an organism disappears from existence.

Some animals become extinct because of natural changes in their environment; others because of human activities, including the effects of hunting, fishing, farming, pollution, and the use of pesticides. Among extinct species are Steller's sea cow, the great auk, the Carolina parakeet, and the dodo. The dodo was a large flightless bird of the island of Mauritius, in the Indian Ocean. It was wiped out in the 17th century.

epiphyte—orchid

fore gets its nutrients and water from the air and rain. An epiphyte usually grows on another plant, not as a parasite but for physical support. Orchids, Spanish moss, and most bromeliads are epiphytes. They are sometimes called *air plants*.

epiphytic Of, relating to, or being an epiphyte.

estivate To become and remain torpid during the summer months. Frogs estivate to avoid high summer temperatures and jerboas may estivate if food is scarce in summer. *Compare* **hibernate**.

estrus The regularly recurring period of sexual receptivity in most female mammals during which mating and conception are likely. *Compare* **rut.**

evergreen forest A forest of the temperate zone composed chiefly of coniferous trees. Also, a tropical rain forest is sometimes called an evergreen forest, because it has green foliage perpetually in evidence.

extinct No longer existing. *See* **extinction** above.

family A category of biological classification of related animals or plants that is the major subdivision of an order and usually includes a number of genera.

fledge (In a young bird) to grow the feathers necessary to attain flight.

fledgling A young bird that has grown the

Food Chain

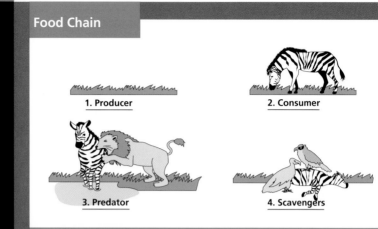

1. Producer
2. Consumer
3. Predator
4. Scavengers

Grassland ecosystem

In a community of organisms there are complex feeding interdependencies. These can be simplified into a food chain to understand how dependencies evolve. For example, in a grassland community the grass is fed upon by a grazing zebra. The zebra itself becomes food for a lion. Scavenging birds consume carrion left from the lion's meal—and the lion itself when it dies.

feathers needed for flight.

food web The total system of overlapping food chains in an ecological community.

forage (Of an animal) to go about in search of food. Also, the food that an animal acquires by foraging.

forest floor The surface that underlies the trees of a forest. The soil layer is often overlaid with decaying vegetation, animal dung, and other forest litter that incorporates into the soil as it decomposes.

G

genera Plural of *genus*.

genus A category of biological classification of organisms that ranks below a family and is usually made up of one or more species.

gestation The period during which young mammals are carried and develop in the womb. Length of the period varies for different species of mammals. For example, coyotes have a gestation period of two months; elephants have one of nearly two years.

grasslands Large tracts of land on which perennial grasses are the dominant vegetation.

grazing animal An animal that feeds chiefly on grasses and other low-growing herbs. Sheep, buffalo, zebras, cattle, and wildebeests are examples of grazing animals.

great apes Members of the family Pongidae, the large apes, including gorillas, orangutans, and chimpanzees but not gibbons, which are of Hylobatidae.

guard hairs Long, coarse hairs on the coat

of some mammals that protect and insulate the softer, denser undercoat. Raccoons, fur seals, musk oxen, beavers, caribou, and mountain goats are examples of mammals having guard hairs.

habitat The natural environment or location in which an animal or plant characteristically lives.

hackles The hairs or feathers along the neck and back of an animal that can stand upright when the animal is angry or threatened.

Hagenbeck, Carl (1844–1913) A German circus director and animal trainer. In 1907 he established the first zoo exhibits without bars, cages, and fences, using instead moats and natural-looking artificial rock walls to restrict the animals.

herbivore An herbivorous animal.

herbivorous Feeding on plants as the main

herbivorous—giraffe

source of food. Cattle, sheep, antelopes, horses, and giraffes are among the herbivorous mammals.

herd A group of animals of one or more species living and moving about together as a social unit; also, to gather, move, and feed together as a herd. Grazing animals like

Hibernation

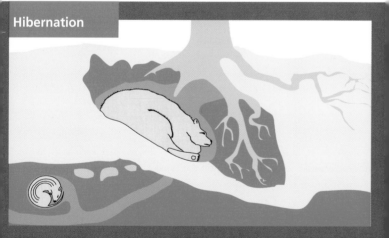

An animal that passes the winter in a torpid or dormant condition is in hibernation. A hibernating animal typically undergoes a lowering of body temperature and a slowing of breathing and metabolism. It survives by using energy stored in its body fat. Warm-blooded animals that hibernate or are in a dormant state in winter include bears, bats, and squirrels. Cold-blooded hibernators include toads, turtles, lizards, and snakes. *Compare* **estivation**.

wildebeest, buffalo, and zebra herd together in large groups for mutual protection in the open African savanna.

hibernate To pass the winter in a torpid or dormant condition as an adaptation for coping with cold weather and dwindling food supplies. A hibernating animal typically undergoes a lowering of body temperature and a slowing of breathing and metabolism. The animal survives by using energy stored in its body fat. *Compare* **estivate**.

hibernation *See* page 217.

home range The area throughout which an animal normally lives and conducts its daily activities. The size of a home range depends on various factors.

hoofed animal An ungulate.

host An organism on which a parasite lives and on whose resources it feeds. Parasites are harmful to their hosts. *See* **parasite**.

humus The dark brown or black organic top layer of soil. It is pro-

duced by the decomposition of plant or animal matter.

immersion exhibit

immersion exhibit A zoo exhibit in which a path for visitors typically passes through and is surrounded by the exhibit. Various means such as natural and artificial plant life, water, artificial rock outcroppings, and sound effects are used to re-create the environment of specific animals. Immersion exhibits help zoo visitors see the relationship between animals and their surroundings.

imprinting A rapid form of learning that occurs in young animals of some species. It is restricted to a short, sensitive period, and frequently concerns learning to follow parents or to recognize characteristics of the parent species or place of birth.

inbreeding Breeding

among closely related individuals, as within a small population.

incubate (Of a bird) to sit on eggs until they hatch. The warmth of the sitting bird's body is essential for the development of the chick. In some bird species both the male and the female parents incubate the eggs; in others, only one parent bird does so.

International Species Inventory System (ISIS) A computerized system by which genetically diverse matches can be arranged between animals from different zoos.

invertebrate—mealworms

invertebrate Any animal, such as an ant, worm, or clam, that lacks a spinal column, or backbone.

ISIS *See* **International Species Inventory System.**

keratin A tough protein substance that is the chemical basis of the horny tissue of which nails, hooves, horns, claws, hair, and feathers consist.

kingdom The highest and most inclusive of the categories of biological classification, ranking above the phylum. Animals and plants each occupy a kingdom.

kit A young offspring of a small fur-bearing animal, such as a fox or beaver.

krill Small shrimplike crustaceans that live in southern oceans in great numbers and are a staple diet of animals such as blue whales, seals, penguins, and albatrosses.

L

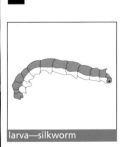

larva—silkworm

larva The immature form, hatching from the eggs of some organisms, that differs considerably in appearance and ecol-

ogy from the sexually mature adult. In insects, the larvae are a wingless feeding stage. They hatch from eggs, and in appearance usually resemble worms. They finally undergo a metamorphosis, or series of physical changes, to become adult insects.

larvae A plural of *larva.*

life cycle The series of developmental stages through which an organism passes during its lifetime.

litter The offspring produced at one birth by an animal that typically produces more than one offspring at a time.

lower canopy The hot and humid layer of the tropical forest that is about 20 feet (6 m) beneath the canopy and above the forest floor. Less dense than the canopy, the lower canopy is formed by saplings, vines, trees, and palms that are adapted to the low intensity of the light. Also called *understory.*

lowland forest Forest growing on areas in the lowlands of a region, usually adjacent to rivers and streams. A lowland

tropical forest is typically hot and humid.

M

Mammalia A class of animals comprising all mammals, including humans. *See* Mammal, page 220.

mangrove forest A type of forest near a coastal area, as at the mouth of the Ganges River in India. A mangrove forest is comprised primarily of mangrove trees, which have intertwining roots like stilts. These roots impede tidal and river currents, thereby allowing sediment to accumulate and stabilize the banks of the watercourse.

mark (By a mammal) to identify a territory by urinating, defecating, depositing secretions from scent glands, or making scratch marks on trees. Such marking establishes the identity of the animal or the limits of the territory being claimed.

marsupial Any of an order of mammals whose newborn young complete their development while being carried

Mammal

Gorilla nursing her babies

Any warm-blooded animal of the class Mammalia, which includes humans. Mammals have a backbone and skin that is more or less covered with hair, and they nourish their young with milk secreted by the mammary glands of the female. There are approximately 4,070 species of mammals, divided into 18 orders. The reign of mammals as the dominant life form on Earth began over 100 million years ago.

in a pouch containing milk glands. The pouch is located on the mother's abdomen. Kangaroos, wombats, and opossums are marsupials.

matriarch A dominant female leader of a group of animals living and moving together. A herd of elephants is led by a matriarch.

meat eater A carnivorous animal.

metabolism The process of building up and breaking down chemical complexes that occurs in the cells of all organisms to produce energy. *Metabolic rate* is the rate at which this process takes place.

microclimate The climate of a restricted or confined habitat, such as a cave, glacier, or burrow, where temperature and humidity may be different from that of the surrounding area.

migrate To travel, especially periodically, from one area or climate to another, usually to breed or to search for food. Birds, mammals, fish, and insects all have species that migrate.

migration The act or process of migrating.

molt—bactrian camel

molt To shed fur, feathers, skin, horns, or shell before replacing with new growth, in a process of periodic renewal; also, the act or process of molting, or the material shed during molting.

mustelid—weasel

mustelid Any mammal of the weasel family Mustelidae, including weasels, minks, otters, skunks, badgers, and wolverines. Mustelids have characteristic musty scents.

N

native Growing or living naturally and typically in a particular locality, as animals that are *native* to arctic regions or plant life *native* to rain forests.

natural selection The natural process by which organisms with traits that are best adapted to a specific environment will survive and reproduce most successfully, thus perpetuating those traits in successive generations and producing evolutionary change.

nestling A bird that is too young to leave its nest.

niche The special role or place in an ecological community occupied by an organism, species, or population, especially in relation to its activities, food, and living requirements.

night vision—slow loris

night vision The ability to see well in very dim light. Many owls have excellent night vision.

nocturnal (Of an animal) active only or chiefly at night.

nomadic Roaming habitually from place to place in search of food and water. Some desert antelope are nomadic animals.

O

olfactory Of or relating to the sense of smell.

omnivore An omnivorous animal.

omnivorous Feeding on both animal and plant matter.

opposable thumb—human

opposable thumb—monkey

opposable thumb A thumb that is capable of being placed against any of the other digits of a hand or foot. Primates have opposable thumbs.

order A category of biological classification of organisms that ranks lower than a class but above a family. Orders are sometimes subdivided into suborders.

overgrazing Grazing of land by livestock or other grazing animals to such an extent that the vegetation cover is damaged or destroyed.

P Q

pack animal A mammal, such as a llama, used for carrying loads.

pampas The vast, virtually treeless grasslands found in parts of southern South America, especially Argentina.

parasite—Rocky Mountain wood tick

parasite An organism that lives in or on and draws sustenance from another organism. The relationship is normally harmful to the host. *See* **host.**

permafrost A permanently frozen layer of subsoil found in the tundra.

photoperiodism An organism's response to its daily periods of exposure to light and darkness, especially as it affects the organism's behavior and development.

photosynthesis A process by which carbohydrates are made from carbon dioxide and water in the chlorophyll-containing tissues of plants exposed to light.

plain or **plains** A broad area of relatively flat, treeless land.

pollinator An agent, such as an animal or bird, that aids in the pollination of plants.

population A group of organisms of the same species inhabiting a particular locality.

prairie A broad tract of level or gently rolling treeless grassland.

predation The capture and eating of prey animals by predators.

predator An animal that lives by hunting and consuming prey animals.

Pollination

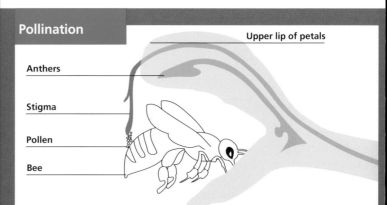

Upper lip of petals

Anthers

Stigma

Pollen

Bee

Lower lip of petals

Pollination is the transfer of pollen from the anthers to the stigmas of flowers. Bees, bats, birds, and other animals, as well as wind and water, aid in pollinating plants.

The transfer of pollen from the anther of one flower to the stigma of another is called *cross-pollination*. The transfer of pollen within the same flower is

called *self-pollination*. Oats, peas, beans, wheat, and cotton are self-pollinating plants. Botanists engage in cross-pollination of plants to create new varieties.

prehensile Adapted for curling around something in order to grasp and hold it. Some monkeys have a prehensile tail that serves as a fifth limb for holding onto tree branches. The black rhino has a prehensile upper lip.

prey animal An animal that is hunted and eaten by a predator.

pride The social unit of lions, consisting of up to 12 related females and up to 6 males. The number of lions in a pride is usually determined by the size and number of prey available in the habitat.

primate

primate Any mammal of the order Primates, which includes humans, apes, monkeys, bush babies, lemurs, lorises, and tarsiers.

quarry Any animal that is hunted for food by a predator.

rain forest A tropical forest having tall, broad-leaved evergreen trees that form a canopy, and an annual rainfall of at least 100 inches (254 cm). Also, a forest in the temperate zone having a variety of kinds of trees, with one or two species dominating, and a heavy annual rainfall.

range The geographical area over which a species is distributed.

raptor A bird of prey. The word *raptor* is from a Latin word meaning "one who seizes."

regenerative Capable of growing anew. Some lizards have regenerative tails that will grow again if the lizard loses its original tail.

regurgitate—penguins

regurgitate To cast up incompletely digested food from the stomach or crop. Some birds, such as hornbills, regur-

gitate food to feed their young.

reintroduction The process of returning animals to their natural habitat after they have been raised elsewhere. Zoos breed endangered species for reintroduction to their natural habitats when conditions there permit it. The process may involve some deliberate "training" of the animal to enable it to cope with its new life.

retractable claws Claws, such as those of many cats, that can be drawn back into the pads of the feet, as well as extended for use.

rodent *See* page 224.

ruminant Any hoofed, even-toed mammal of the suborder Ruminantia, including cows, goats, sheep, deer, camels, and giraffes, that ruminate their food and possess a three- or four-chambered stomach.

ruminate To chew again food that has been chewed once, swallowed, and returned to the mouth; to chew the cud.

rut A periodically recurring state of sexual ex-

Rodent

Ground squirrel

Any small gnawing mammal of the order Rodentia. Rodents have four chisel-shaped teeth called *incisors*, one pair in the upper jaw and one in the lower. These teeth continue to grow as the animal's gnawing wears them down, and therefore last for the animal's lifetime. The largest rodents are the capybaras of South America; mice are the smallest. Some other rodents are beavers, rats, squirrels, chipmunks, hamsters, gerbils, muskrats, porcupines, gophers, and lemmings.

citement in the male of some mammals, such as deer or sheep. *Compare* **estrus.**

S

savanna Grassland of tropical or subtropical areas that is marked by scattered trees and undergrowth resistant to seasonal drought.

scat The fecal droppings of animals.

scavenge To feed on carrion or garbage. Vultures are scavengers.

scent gland A gland in some animals, such as beavers, weasels, otters, or white-tailed deer, that secretes a distinctive odor for marking territory.

scent mark A distinctive odor, as from urine or the secretion of a scent gland, that an animal uses to mark its territory. Such an odor may not be detectable by humans.

semiarid Having relatively low rainfall—about 10 to 20 inches (25–51 cm) each year.

semidesert A dry region that has a semiarid climate, less arid than that of a desert, and sparse vegetation.

silverback A mature male gorilla, having silvery white hair that appears across its back.

small cats—ocelot

small cats Any of the members of the cat family that are smaller than the big cats and belong to the genus *Felis*. The small cats include cougars, lynxes, bobcats, ocelots, wildcats, and domestic cats.

specialist hunter A mammal, such as a cheetah, specialized for preying on a particular kind of quarry. It may be so reliant on one kind of prey animal that its survival is threatened if that animal becomes scarce.

species The basic category of biological classification of organisms below genus or subgenus. Members of a species look alike and are able to mate successfully with one another. A species may be further divided into subspecies and varieties.

Species Survival Plans (SSPs) A program carried out by zoos in the United States and other countries that coordinates breeding arrangements to increase the population of a species. More than 50 species of endangered or threatened animals are covered by SSPs, and many have been successfully returned to their natural habitat as a result.

SSPs *See* **Species Survival Plans.**

stag An adult male deer.

steppe Any of the vast, essentially treeless plains of grassland found in parts of southeastern Europe and western and southwestern Asia.

stereoscopic vision Vision, as in all primates including humans, that allows things to be seen three-dimensionally.

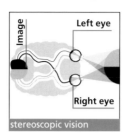
stereoscopic vision

subgenus A category of biological classification of organisms that is below a genus and above a species.

suborder A category of biological classification between an order and a family.

subspecies A category of biological classification of organisms that is a subdivision of a species.

symbiosis A close, interdependent relationship between two organisms of different species.

symbiotic Of, relating to, or characteristic of symbiosis.

taiga *See* **boreal forest**.

talon A claw, especially

of a bird of prey, such as a hawk, owl, or eagle.

talon—sparrowhawk

tapetum lucidum A layer of tissue in the back of the eye of some mammals, such as cats and weasels, that reflects light in such a way as to intensify the animal's night vision. The presence of the tapetum lucidum will cause the animal's eyes to glow at night when reflecting light from a flashlight or other light source.

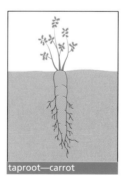
taproot—carrot

taproot A main root, as of a tree, that grows downward and produces smaller roots that grow off to the side.

temperate Having or marked by a moderate climate that is typically marked by seasonal change.

territorial (In an animal) disposed or ready to occupy and defend a territory.

territory The geographical area that an animal or a group of animals defends against intrusion by other animals, especially of the same species.

testosterone A male sex hormone that, when increased to a certain level in an adult male deer or elk, triggers its period of rut.

threatened species A species whose somewhat precarious chances for survival expose it to becoming an endangered species. *See* **endangered species.**

timberline The highest limit at which trees will grow in the high altitudes of mountainous regions. Also called *tree line.*

torpid Being sluggish or inactive, as an animal that is hibernating or estivating.

toxin A poisonous substance produced in an organism, such as a poison-arrow frog, as a means of defense.

tree line *See* **timberline.**

troop A group of animals, such as monkeys, living and moving about together.

tropical forest Any forest in a tropical region.

tundra Any of the vast, fairly level, treeless plains found in the arctic regions of North America, Europe, and Asia. Tundras are cold and dry.

Vertebrate

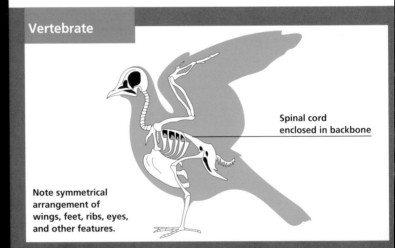

Spinal cord enclosed in backbone

Note symmetrical arrangement of wings, feet, ribs, eyes, and other features.

Any animal with a spinal column, or backbone, enclosing the spinal cord. Mammals, birds, reptiles, amphibians, and fish are all vertebrates. The vertebrate body is characteristically marked by *bilateral symmetry,* which means that the right and left sides of the body are mirror images. There are about 40,000 species of vertebrates, divisible into 8 classes.

U V

underfur A mammal's undercoat of dense, soft fur that is protected by guard hairs.

understory *See* **lower canopy.**

ungulate—Asian elephant

ungulate Any of the even- and odd-toed hoofed mammals, including cattle, swine, horses, camels, rhinoceroses, hippopotamuses, tapirs, and elephants.

veld Open grasslands with scattered shrubs and trees, characteristic of parts of southern Africa. This word is often spelled *veldt.*

venom A poisonous substance secreted by an animal and usually transmitted by sting or bite. Animals that produce venom include scorpions, certain snakes and spiders, a few species of lizard, and two mammals— the adult male platypus and one species of shrew.

vertebrate *See* page 226.

vocalization A sound produced by the passage of air through various anatomical structures in air-breathing animals. Amphibians, reptiles, birds, and mammals all vocalize.

W X Y Z

warm-blooded Having a constant, relatively high body temperature independent of the surrounding environment. Mammals and birds are warm-blooded. *See also* **cold-blooded.**

wetlands Low-lying, water-saturated areas of land, such as marshes, swamps, and bogs. Wading birds and waterfowl often inhabit wetlands.

zygodactyl— double-eyed fig parrot

zygodactyl Having two toes pointed forward and two backward. Some birds, such as parrots, have zygodactyl feet that enable them to grasp objects firmly.

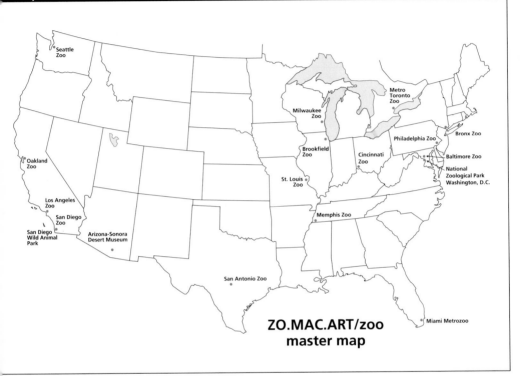

Seattle Zoo

Metro Toronto Zoo

Milwaukee Zoo

Brookfield Zoo

Cincinnati Zoo

Philadelphia Zoo

Bronx Zoo

Baltimore Zoo

National Zoological Park Washington, D.C.

Oakland Zoo

St. Louis Zoo

Los Angeles Zoo

San Diego Zoo

Memphis Zoo

San Diego Wild Animal Park

Arizona-Sonora Desert Museum

San Antonio Zoo

Miami Metrozoo

**ZO.MAC.ART/zoo
master map**

Zoos Across North America

The eighteen zoos shown on the following pages represent the diversity of the 162 zoos in North America accredited by the American Zoo and Aquarium Association. Zoos often expand or change their habitats; therefore, visitors may want to contact individual zoos for updated information before planning a visit.

Zoo Maps

Key to Animals

antelopes	lions/cats
bears	monkeys
bison/buffalo	otters
camels	parrots
chimpanzees	penguins
deer	puffins
eagles/hawks	reptiles
elephants	rhinos
giraffes	seals/sea lions
gorillas	sheep
hippos	pelicans/storks
horse	tigers
kangaroos	tortoises
koala	water birds
llamas	wolves/foxes
	zebras

Arizona-Sonora Desert Museum

Arizona-Sonora Desert Museum
2021 North Kinney Road
Tucson, Arizona 85743
(602) 883-1380

Established 1952

Over 300 species of animals and 1,300 kinds of plants are on exhibit. The displays throughout the museum are designed to show how plants, animals, and people coexist in the Sonora Desert region. Recent additions are the Desert Grasslands and the expanded Hummingbirds of the Sonoran Desert Region exhibit.

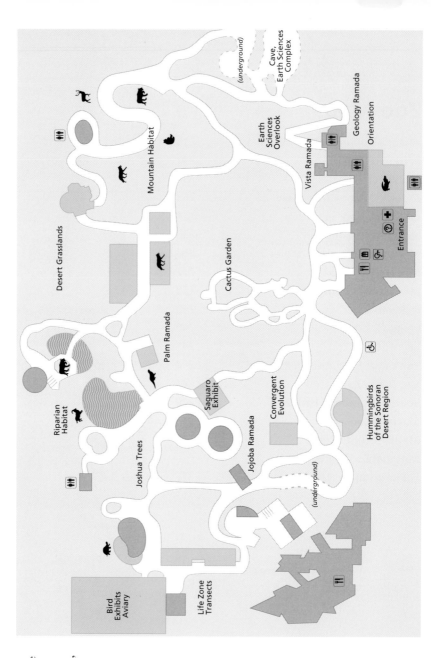

- Desert Grasslands
- Mountain Habitat
- Cave, Earth Sciences Complex *(underground)*
- Earth Sciences Overlook
- Geology Ramada
- Orientation
- Vista Ramada
- Cactus Garden
- Entrance
- Palm Ramada
- Riparian Habitat
- Saguaro Exhibit
- Convergent Evolution
- Hummingbirds of the Sonoran Desert Region
- Joshua Trees
- Jojoba Ramada
- Bird Exhibits Aviary
- Life Zone Transects
- *(underground)*

Legend:
- ☐ footpaths
- ☐ people buildings
- ☐ animal buildings
- ☐ parking areas
- ☐ grassy areas
- ☐ water
- ♿ access
- ⓘ information
- 🍴 restaurant/café
- ✚ first aid
- 🚻 restrooms
- 🎁 gift shop

Baltimore Zoo
Druid Hill Park
Baltimore, MD 21217
(410) 366-5466 (366-LION)

Established 1876

The third oldest zoo in the United States, its 200-acre park houses more than 1,200 mammals, birds, and reptiles. It also contains one of the finest zoo hospitals in the nation. In 1995, visitors will be able to enjoy two new exhibits, Leopards' Lair and Chimpanzee Forest.

African Village

Leopards' Lair

Chimpanzee Forest

African Watering Hole

Children's Zoo

Maryland Wilderness

Entrance

Maryland Building Administrative

Mansion House Administrative

☐ footpaths
☐ people buildings
☐ animal buildings
☐ parking areas
☐ grassy areas
☐ water
☎ phone
♿ access
🅿 parking
🍴 restaurant/café
✚ first aid
🚻 restrooms
🎁 gift shop
monorail
tram

Bronx Zoo
2300 Southern Blvd
Bronx, NY 10460
(718) 220-5100

Established 1895

The largest metropolitan wildlife park in the United States, the zoo displays over 700 different species on 265 acres. Special exhibits include Jungleworld and The World of Birds, which features 327 species of birds.

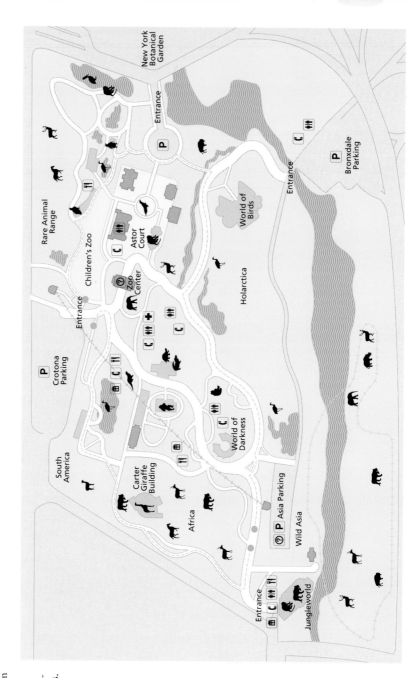

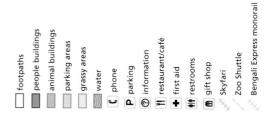

- footpaths
- people buildings
- animal buildings
- parking areas
- grassy areas
- water
- ☎ phone
- P parking
- ⓘ information
- ✺ restaurant/café
- ✚ first aid
- restrooms
- gift shop
- Skyfari
- Zoo Shuttle
- Bengali Express monorail

Brookfield Zoo
3300 Golf Road
Brookfield, IL 60513
(708) 485-0263

Established 1934

Chicago's 215 acre Brookfield Zoo is home to 2,500 animals in seven different exhibition areas. Naturalistic exhibits include Habitat Africa!, a re-creation of an African reserve that displays diverse plant and animal life.

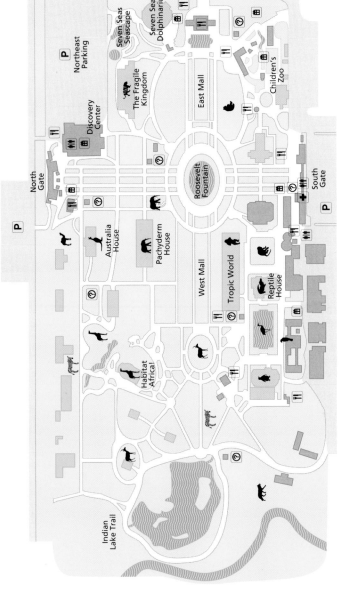

Seven Seas Seascape

Seven Seas Dolphinarium

Northeast Parking

The Fragile Kingdom

East Mall

Children's Zoo

Discovery Center

North Gate

Roosevelt Fountain

South Gate

Australia House

Pachyderm House

West Mall

Tropic World

Reptile House

Habitat Africa!

Indian Lake Trail

footpaths
people buildings
animal buildings
parking areas
grassy areas
water
P parking
information
restaurant/café
first aid
restrooms
gift shop

Cincinnati Zoo

Cincinnati Zoo (and botanical garden),
3400 Vine Street
Cincinnati, OH
45220-1399
(513) 281-4701

Established 1875

Over one million visitors come each year to see more than 750 different types of animals and 3,000 plants. Exhibits include the Cat House, Gorilla World, which houses a large Silverback gorilla, and the World of Insects.

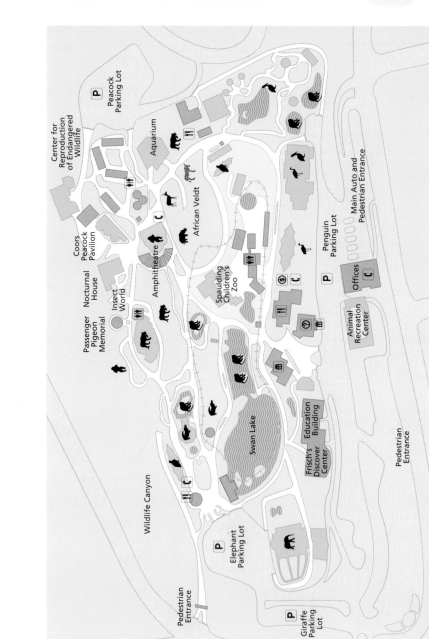

Legend

- ☐ footpaths
- people buildings
- animal buildings
- parking areas
- grassy areas
- water
- ☎ phone
- P parking
- ? information
- ❙❙ restaurant/café
- restrooms
- $ bank machine
- gift shop
- train

Map labels:

Center for Reproduction of Endangered Wildlife

Peacock Parking Lot

P

Aquarium

Coors Peacock Pavilion

African Veltd

Amphitheatre

Nocturnal House

Insect World

Passenger Pigeon Memorial

Spaulding Children's Zoo

Penguin Parking Lot

Main Auto and Pedestrian Entrance

Offices

Animal Recreation Center

Pedestrian Entrance

Wildlife Canyon

Swan Lake

Frisch's Discover Center

Education Building

Elephant Parking Lot

Pedestrian Entrance

Giraffe Parking Lot

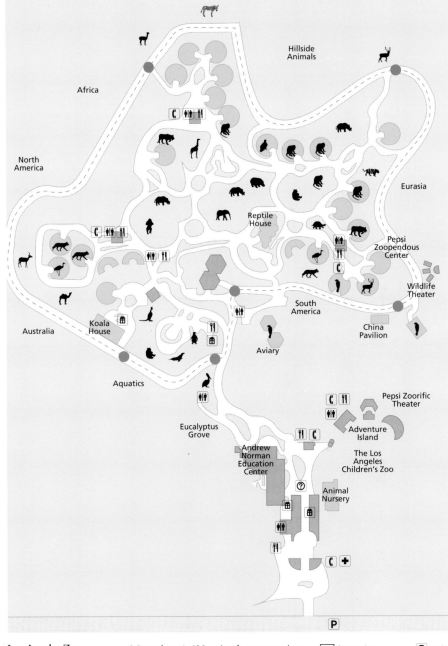

Los Angeles Zoo
5333 Zoo Drive
Los Angeles, CA 90027
(213) 666-4090

Established 1966

More than 1,600 animals representing 400 different species are housed on 80 acres. The zoo is divided into five areas by continent. The Los Angeles Zoo has very successful breeding programs, including the hatching and rearing of California Condors.

☐ footpaths	**P** parking
▨ people buildings	⊙ information
▨ animal buildings	¶¶ restaurant/café
▨ parking areas	✚ first aid
☐ grassy areas	♦♦ restrooms
▨ water	🏠 gift shop
C phone	⁄ Safari Shuttle

Memphis Zoo

Memphis Zoo
2000 Galloway Street
Memphis, TN 38112
(901) 725-3400

Established 1906

Home to over 2,800 animals representing more than 400 species, a renovation plan is underway to provide more natural habitats on its 80 acres. The first of its new exhibits is a display of some of the world's finest wild cats.

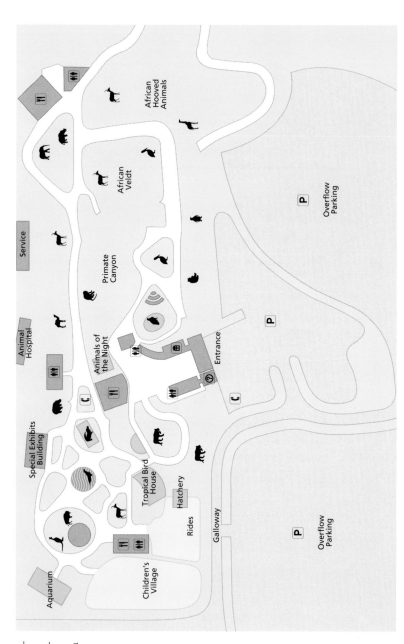

African Hooved Animals

African Veldt

Service

Primate Canyon

Animal Hospital

Animals of the Night

Entrance

Special Exhibits Building

Tropical Bird House

Hatchery

Rides

Galloway

Overflow Parking

Overflow Parking

Children's Village

Aquarium

- footpaths
- people buildings
- animal buildings
- parking areas
- grassy areas
- water
- phone
- P parking
- information
- restaurant/café
- restrooms
- gift shop
- monorail

End of Path

Boat Rides

Kids' Fun Center

Concert Meadow

Amphitheatre

Australia

Wings of Asia

Special Events Area

Classrooms

Metrozoo Administration Building

Entrance

Ecology Theatre

Petting Zoo

Zoological Society Administration

East Parking Lot

West Parking Lot

Miami Metrozoo
12400 SW 152nd Street
Miami, FL 33177
(305) 251-0403

Established 1980

Metrozoo encompasses 24 acres, with 500 acres for expansion. The animal collection consists of 900 animals representing 260 species of reptiles, birds, and mammals. Metrozoo has received numerous awards for the breeding of animals, including one for its crocodilian captive breeding program.

footpaths
people buildings
animal buildings
parking areas
grassy areas
water
phone
access

parking
information
restaurant/café
first aid
restrooms
bank machine
gift shop
monorail

Milwaukee County Zoo

Milwaukee County Zoo
10001 West Bluemound Rd.
Milwaukee, WI 53266
(414) 771-5500

Established 1958

Over 2,500 animals are exhibited on 200 acres. Exhibits include Primates of the World and a naturalistic exhibit which shows animals in predator/prey settings. A new exhibit shows nineteen robotic, life-like dinosaurs in a setting that resembles the earth millions of years ago.

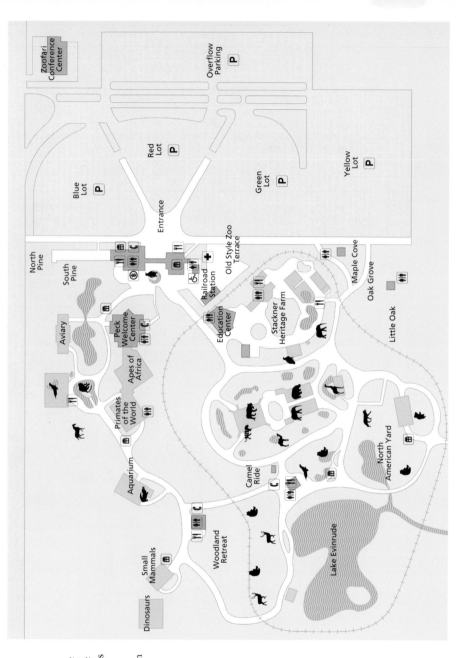

- ☐ footpaths
- ☐ people buildings
- ☐ animal buildings
- ☐ parking areas
- ☐ grassy areas
- 〜 water
- ☎ phone
- ♿ access
- 🅿 parking
- ⊘ information
- 🍴 restaurant/café
- ✚ first aid
- 🚻 restrooms
- $ bank machine
- 🏧 gift shop
- ╳╳ railroad

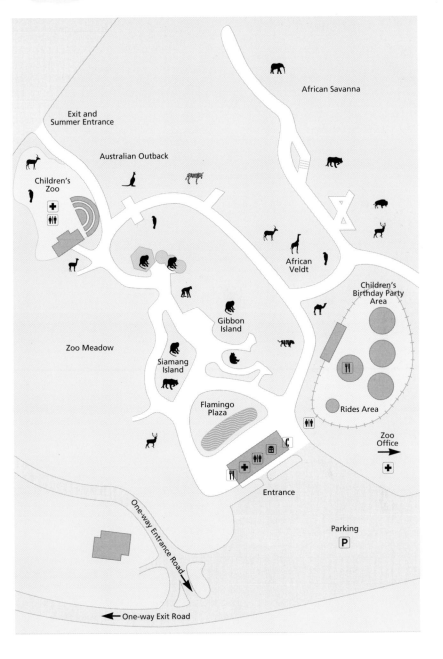

African Savanna

Exit and
Summer Entrance

Australian Outback

Children's
Zoo

Zoo Meadow

African
Veldt

Gibbon
Island

Siamang
Island

Children's
Birthday Party
Area

Flamingo
Plaza

Rides Area

Zoo
Office

Entrance

One-way Entrance Road

Parking

← One-way Exit Road

Oakland Zoo
977 Golf Links Road
Oakland, Ca 94605
(510) 632-9523

Established 1922

A renovation and expansion program focuses on three major areas: Tropical Rainforests of the World, the African Savanna, and California 1820. New exhibits have been added to the park, including the Black Rhino exhibit and Siamang Island.

☐ footpaths	P parking
▪ people buildings	⑦ information
▪ animal buildings	¶ restaurant/café
▪ parking areas	✚ first aid
☐ grassy areas	♙ restrooms
～ water	⑤ bank machine
C phone	⊞ gift shop
♿ access	⨯⨯ train

Philadelphia Zoo
3400 West Girard Avenue
Philadelphia, Pennsylvania 19104-1191
(215) 243-1100

Established 1859

The oldest zoo in the United States, its 42 acres are home to over 1,500 animals. Along with some of the best examples of American zoo architecture, special attractions include rare white lions in the Lion House, and diving polar bears in Bear Country.

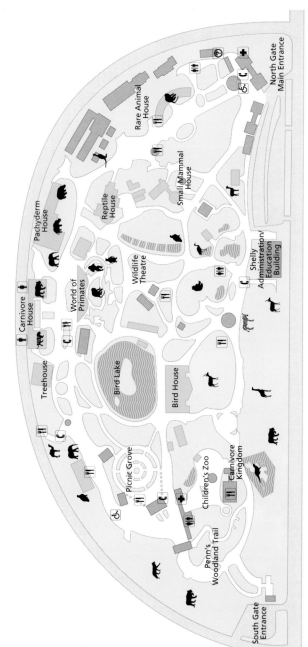

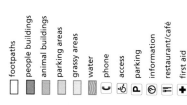

- footpaths
- people buildings
- animal buildings
- parking areas
- grassy areas
- water
- phone
- access
- parking
- information
- restaurant/café
- first aid
- restrooms
- bank machine
- gift shop

Rift Valley Track

Forest Trail

Australian Aviary

Australian Walkabout

Service Area

Playground

Theater of Birds

Nursery

Service Area

Aquarium

Children's Zoo

Playground

Education Center

Animal Arena

Service Area

Exit

Tickets

Office

San Antonio Zoo
3903 N. St. Mary's Street
San Antonio, TX
78212-3199
(210) 734-7183

Established 1924

Home to over 3,000 animals representing 700 species, the zoo includes an Australian Walkabout and an exhibit of Africa's Rift Valley. Also displayed is the first white rhino born in the United States, and the only exhibit of the endangered whooping crane.

☐ footpaths
◼ people buildings
◼ animal buildings
▨ parking areas
☐ grassy areas
〰 water
☏ phone
♿ access

P parking
ⓘ information
🍴 restaurant/café
✚ first aid
🚻 restrooms
🎁 gift shop

San Diego Wild Animal Park

San Diego Wild Animal Park
15500 San Pasqual Valley Rd
Escondido CA, 92027-9614
(619) 234-6541

Established 1972

Over 3,000 birds and mammals are displayed on its 2,200 acres. Described as "a zoo unlike any zoo," it is designed primarily for the animals, which are allowed to roam about in herds and flocks. Major attractions are the Hidden Jungle exhibit and the Kilimanjaro Hiking Trail.

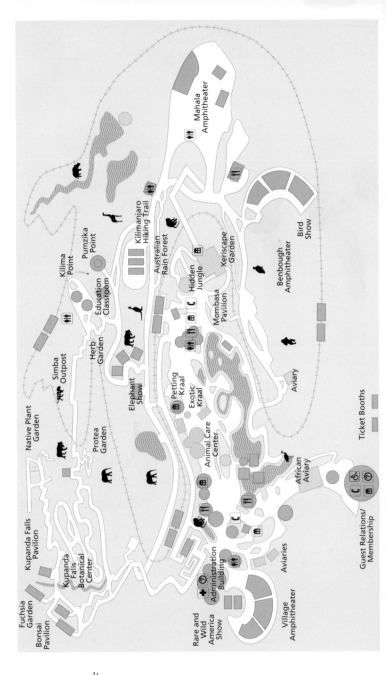

Legend

- footpaths
- people buildings
- animal buildings
- parking areas
- grassy areas
- water
- phone
- information
- restaurant/café
- first aid
- restrooms
- gift shop
- monorail

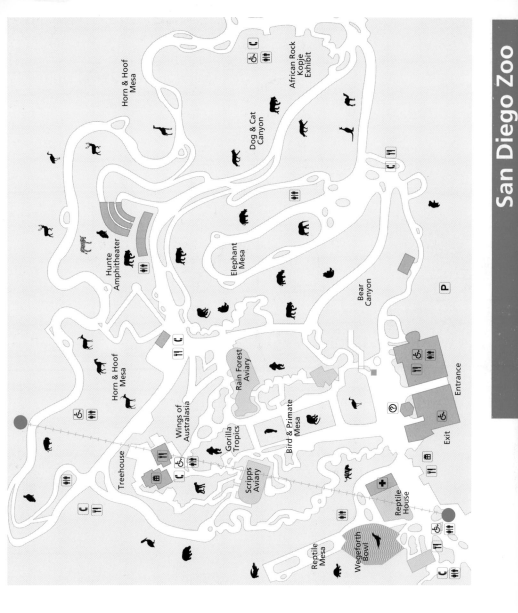

San Diego Zoo
P.O. Box 551
San Diego, CA
92112-0551
(619) 234-3153

Established 1922

Located in a 100 acre tropical garden, the zoo displays 4,000 animals from 800 species, including the largest collection of parrots and parrot-like birds in the U.S. Other rare animals include the Sichuan takin (related to musk oxen) from China and Przewalski's horse from Mongolia.

Horn & Hoof Mesa

African Rock Kopie Exhibit

Dog & Cat Canyon

Horn & Hoof Mesa

Hunte Amphitheater

Elephant Mesa

Bear Canyon

Horn & Hoof Mesa

Rain Forest Aviary

Wings of Australasia

Gorilla Tropics

Bird & Primate Mesa

Treehouse

Scripps Aviary

Entrance

Exit

Reptile Mesa

Wegeforth Bowl

Reptile House

footpaths

people buildings

animal buildings

parking areas

grassy areas

water

☎ phone

♿ access

P parking

🛈 information

🍽 restaurant/café

✚ first aid

🚻 restrooms

🏛 gift shop

≋ Skyfari

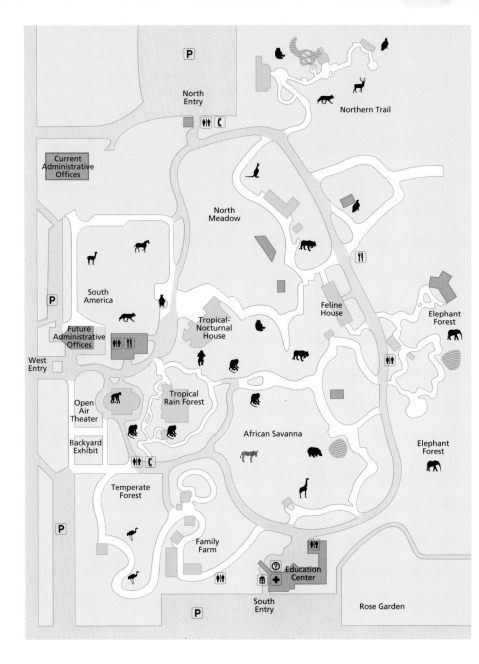

North Entry

Northern Trail

P

Current Administrative Offices

North Meadow

South America

P

Future Administrative Offices

West Entry

Open Air Theater

Backyard Exhibit

Tropical Rain Forest

Tropical-Nocturnal House

Feline House

Elephant Forest

African Savanna

Elephant Forest

Temperate Forest

P

Family Farm

Education Center

South Entry

Rose Garden

P

Woodland Park Zoo
5500 Phinney Avenue North
Seattle, WA 98103-5897
(206) 684-4800
TDD (206) 684-4026

Established 1900

Now featuring 300 species of wildlife on 92 acres, zoo exhibit areas are being redesigned to create eight bioclimatic exhibit zones: African Savanna, Tropical Rain Forest, Tropical Asia, Temperate Forest, Australasia, Northern Trail, Steppe, and Desert.

☐ footpaths	P parking
■ people buildings	⑦ information
■ animal buildings	¶ restaurant/café
■ parking areas	✚ first aid
☐ grassy areas	⚥ restrooms
≋ water	🎁 gift shop
C phone	

Saint Louis Zoo
Forest Park
Saint Louis, MO 63110
(314) 781-0900

Established 1916

The 83-acre zoo began with the 1904 World's Fair and grew into a collection of 6,000 animals. A gigantic walk-through aviary is a main attraction. The Antelope House contains some of the rarest animals in the world.

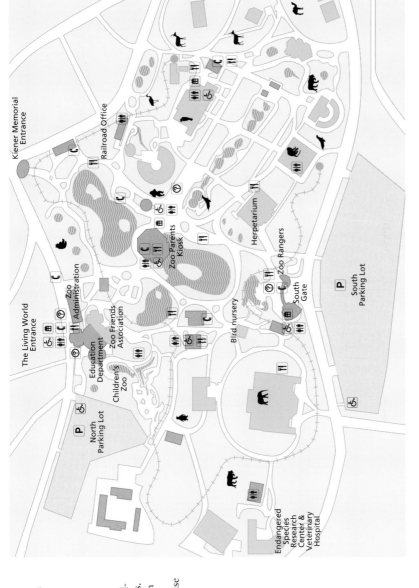

□ footpaths
■ people buildings
■ animal buildings
■ parking areas
■ grassy areas
  water
☎ phone
♿ access
🅿 parking
ℹ information
🍴 restaurant/café
✚ first aid
🚻 restrooms
🎁 gift shop
✕✕✕ railroad

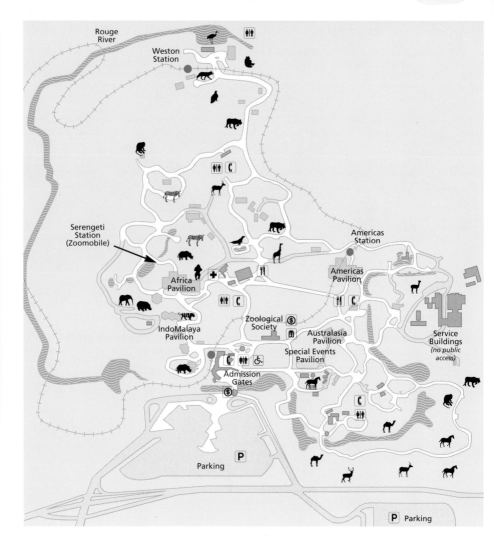

Rouge
River

Weston
Station

Serengeti
Station
(Zoomobile)

Americas
Station

Africa
Pavilion

Americas
Pavilion

IndoMalaya
Pavilion

Zoological
Society

Australasia
Pavilion

Special Events
Pavilion

Service
Buildings
*(no public
access)*

Admission
Gates

Parking

P Parking

Metro Toronto Zoo
P.O. Box 280
West Hill, Ontario
(416) 392-5934

Established 1974

Containing 710 acres and over 5,000 animals, this zoo is designed "zoogeographically," arranging the various plants and animals according to their location in the wild. Color-coded trails throughout the zoo lead visitors to exhibit areas. Special features include the Camel Trail and the Grizzly Bear Trail.

☐ footpaths
▨ people buildings
▨ animal buildings
▨ parking areas
▨ grassy areas
▨ water
C phone
♿ access

P parking
⊙ information
🍴 restaurant/café
✚ first aid
🚻 restrooms
⑤ bank machine
🎁 gift shop
monorail

National Zoological Park
(Smithsonian National Zoo)
3001 Connecticut Ave., NW
Washington, DC 20008
(202) 673-4800

Established 1889

Extending across 163 acres, the zoo's 397 species of animal include the first Komodo dragon hatched outside of Indonesia. Highlighted exhibits include Amazonia, with 358 species of plants and animals, the Reptile Discovery Center, and a unique Invertebrate Exhibit, containing spiders, crabs, octopuses, and sponges.

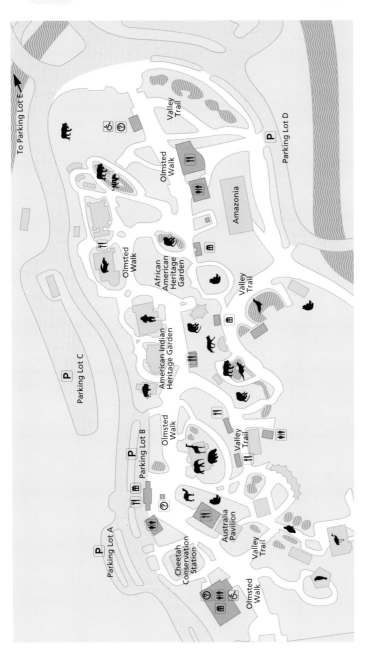

To Parking Lot E

Parking Lot C

Parking Lot B

Parking Lot A

Parking Lot D

Olmsted Walk

Valley Trail

Amazonia

African American Heritage Garden

American Indian Heritage Garden

Australia Pavilion

Cheetah Conservation Station

footpaths

people buildings

animal buildings

parking areas

grassy areas

water

P parking

wheelchairs

information

restaurant/café

restrooms

gift shop

Index

Credits

AA—Animals Animals
ASDM—Arizona-Sonora Desert Museum
*BGT—Busch Gardens Tampa
FRWC—Fossil Rim Wildlife Center
MFW—Maine Department of Inland Fisheries and Wildlife
MMZ—Miami Metrozoo
NPS—National Park Service
NZP—National Zoological Park
NTWP—Northwest Trek Wildlife Park
**SWC—Sea World California
USFWS—U.S. Fish and Wildlife Service
ZSSD—Zoological Society of San Diego

1 Jessie Cohen, NZP; 2–3 Jim Tuten, BGT*; 4–5 Jessie Cohen, NZP; 6–7 USFWS; 11 Wildlife Safari; 13 Ron Magill, MMZ; 17 Jessie Cohen, NZP; 18 Jessie Cohen, NZP (l,r); 19 Jessie Cohen, NZP (t,b); 20 PhotoDisc, Inc.‡ (t), Jessie Cohen, NZP (b); 21 Jessie Cohen, NZP; 22 Ron Magill, MMZ (l), Ron Garrison, © ZSSD (r); 23 Ron Garrison, © ZSSD (l), FRWC (r); 24 © Peter L. Kresan; 25 Jessie Cohen, NZP (t,b); 27 Michael Freeman/West Stock; 30 Jim Tuten, BGT* (t), PhotoDisc, Inc.‡ (b); 31 © ZSSD; 32 Jessie Cohen, NZP; 33 Jim Tuten, BGT* (l), © ZSSD (r); 34 © ZSSD (t), PhotoDisc, Inc.‡ (m), Ron Garrison, © ZSSD (b); 35 Oakland Zoo (t,m), PhotoDisc, Inc.‡ (b); 36 PhotoDisc, Inc.‡ (t), Ron Garrison, © ZSSD (b); 37 PhotoDisc, Inc.‡ (l), Jessie Cohen, NZP (r); 38 © ZSSD (l), Jessie Cohen, NZP (r); 39 Jessie Cohen, NZP (t,b); 40 Jessie Cohen, NZP (l), © ZSSD (r); 41 Milwaukee County Zoo Photo/M. A. Nepper; 42 Jessie Cohen, NZP (l), FRWC (r); 43 Jessie Cohen, NZP (tl,tr), Ron Magill, MMZ (b); 44 PhotoDisc, Inc.‡ (t), Jim Tuten, BGT* (b); 45 AA, © 1995 Richard Packwood (t), AA, © 1995 Mike Birkhead, Oxford Scientific Films (b); 46 Jessie Cohen, NZP (t), Jim Tuten, BGT* (b); 47 Clyde Peeling's Reptiland (l), © ZSSD (r); 48 PhotoDisc, Inc.‡ (t), Clyde Peeling's Reptiland (b); 49 PhotoDisc, Inc.‡ (t), Jessie Cohen, NZP (m,b); 50 Ron Garrison, © ZSSD; 51 Jessie Cohen, NZP; 52 Ron Magill, MMZ (t,b); 53 Ron Garrison, © ZSSD (t,b); 54 © ZSSD; 55 Jessie Cohen, NZP (t), © ZSSD (b); 56 Jessie Cohen, NZP (l), Jim Tuten, BGT* (r); 57 Jim Tuten, BGT* (l), Jessie Cohen, NZP (r); 58 © Linda Schwartz; 59 Jane Ruffin, Philadelphia Zoo (tl), Jessie Cohen, NZP (tr), PhotoDisc, Inc.‡ (b); 60 Jessie Cohen, NZP (tl), Ron Garrison, © ZSSD (tr,b); 61 Jessie Cohen, NZP (t), Ron Garrison, © ZSSD (b); 62 Jessie Cohen, NZP (t), © ZSSD (b); 63 Bob Couey, SWC**; 65 Michael Freeman/West Stock; 66 AA, © 1995 Terry G. Murphy; 67 PhotoDisc, Inc.‡; 68 AA, © 1995 Zig Leszczynski; 69 PhotoDisc, Inc.‡ (t), Wildlife Safari (b); 70 Jessie Cohen, NZP (l), PhotoDisc, Inc.‡ (r); 71 Jim Tuten, BGT* (t), Ron Magill, MMZ (b); 72 Jim Tuten, BGT*; 73 FRWC (t), Ron Magill, MMZ (b); 74 Jim Tuten, BGT* (t,b); 75 PhotoDisc, Inc.‡; 76 Jessie Cohen, NZP (t), Ron Magill, MMZ (b); 77 FRWC (t), Jim Tuten, BGT* (b); 78 © Gene N. Keepers, FRWC; 79 PhotoDisc, Inc.‡; 80 AA, © 1995 Norbert Rosing, Oxford Scientific Films (t), PhotoDisc, Inc.‡ (b); 81 Ron Magill, MMZ (t), Jim Tuten, BGT* (b); 83 Jessie Cohen, NZP (t), Ron Magill, MMZ (b); 84 Bob Couey, SWC** (tl), PhotoDisc, Inc.‡ (tr), Jessie Cohen, NZP (bl,br); 85 PhotoDisc, Inc.‡ (tl), Patricia A. Eynon (tr,bc), © Cass Germany, Houston Zoological Gardens (bl), Jessie Cohen, NZP (br); 86 AA, © 1995 Anupe Manojshan (t), AA, © 1995 E. R. Degginger (m), AA, © 1995 Dale & Marian Zimmerman (b); 87 NPS; 88 Gary Kramer, NTWP; 89 Ron Magill, MMZ (t), NTWP (b); 90 PhotoDisc, Inc.‡ (l), Jessie Cohen, NZP (r); 91 © George Barnett, FRWC (tl), © ZSSD (tc), Jim Tuten, BGT* (tr), James C. Leupold, USFWS (b); 92 PhotoDisc, Inc.‡; 93 Jessie Cohen, NZP (t), Luray Parker, USFWS (b); 94 AA, © 1995 Mark Stouffer (t), © ZSSD (b); 95 Jessie Cohen, NZP (t), © ZSSD (b); 96 Jessie Cohen, NZP (l), Jim Tuten, BGT* (r); 97 Jessie Cohen, NZP; 99 AA, © 1995 Mickey Gibson ; 100 © Peter L. Kresan; 101 San Antonio Zoo (l), © Peter L. Kresan (r); 102 Ken Kelley, © ZSSD (tl,b), Ron Garrison, © ZSSD (tr); 103 AA, © 1995 Mickey Gibson; 104 J. D. Peterson, ASDM (l), © ZSSD (r); 105 Ron Garrison, © ZSSD (t), Dick George, The Phoenix Zoo (b); 106 © ZSSD; 107 AA, © 1995 Ashod Francis (t), AA, © 1995 Michael Fogden (m), Ron Garrison, © ZSSD (b); 108 © ZSSD(l,r); 109 © Peter L.

Kresan (l), ASDM (r); **110** USFWS (t), ASDM (b); **111** © ZSSD; **112** Jessie Cohen, NZP (t), Ron Garrison, © ZSSD (b); **113** Jessie Cohen, NZP (t,b); **114** © ZSSD; **115** © The Living Desert (l), Jessie Cohen, NZP (r); **116** © Peter L. Kresan (t), ASDM (b); **117** ASDM (l), © Peter L. Kresan (r); **118** © The Living Desert; **119** San Antonio Zoo (tl,tr,b); **120** Jessie Cohen, NZP (t,b); **121** © The Living Desert; **122** © ZSSD (l), Jessie Cohen, NZP (r); **123** Dick George, The Phoenix Zoo; **124** © ZSSD; **125** ASDM; **126** Jessie Cohen, NZP (l,r); **127** © ZSSD (tl), Jessie Cohen, NZP (tr), Ron Garrison, © ZSSD (b); **129** Mark Newman/West Stock; **130** PhotoDisc, Inc.‡; **131** Chris Schmitz, NTWP (tl), Bill Cross, MFW (tr), Michael Mauch, NTWP (b); **132** PhotoDisc, Inc.‡; **133** Yosemite Collections, NPS (t), Chris Schmitz, NTWP (b); **134** NPS (l,r); **135** © ZSSD (l,r); **136** Jessie Cohen, NZP (t), PhotoDisc, Inc.‡ (b); **137** Bill Cross, MFW; **138** AA, © 1995 Bates Littlehales (tl), Photo Archives, NZP (tr), Ron Garrison, © ZSSD (b); **139** Jessie Cohen, NZP (l), AA, © 1995 Robert Maier (r); **140** PhotoDisc, Inc.‡ (l), Gary Kramer, NTWP (r); **141** Kent Olson, USFWS (t), PhotoDisc, Inc.‡ (b); **142** Jessie Cohen, NZP; **143** Chris Schmitz, NTWP (t), PhotoDisc, Inc.‡ (b); **144** Jessie Cohen, NZP (tl,tr,br), Photo Archives, NZP (bl); **145** Jessie Cohen, NZP (t,fl,br), Photo Archives, NZP (bl); **146** PhotoDisc, Inc.‡ (l,r); **147** © ZSSD (t,b); **148** ASDM; **149** David Meardon, USFWS; **150** Jessie Cohen, NZP (tl), AA, © 1995 Hans & Judy Beste (tr), AA, © 1995 Leonard Lee Rue III (bl), AA, © 1995 Marty Stouffer Productions (br); **151** AA, © 1995 David C. Fritts (t), Jessie Cohen, NZP (bl), PhotoDisc, Inc.‡ (br); **153** Dean Biggens, USFWS; **154** PhotoDisc, Inc.‡; **155** LaVerne Smith, USFWS; **156** John & Karen Hollingsworth, USFWS; **157** Jessie Cohen, NZP (t), Ron Garrison, © ZSSD (b); **158** AA, © 1995 Robert Maier (t), AA, © 1995 Leonard Lee Rue III (b); **159** AA, © 1995 Gerard Lacz; **160** Jessie Cohen, NZP (t,b); **161** USFWS; **162** Ronald L. Bell, USFWS; **163** NPS (l), Michael Mauch, NTWP (r); **164** PhotoDisc, Inc.‡; **165** W. S. Keller, NPS (t), Bob Stevens, USFWS (b); **166** AA, © 1995 E. R. Degginger (t), © ZSSD (b); **167** AA, © 1995 R. Kolar; **168** Jessie Cohen, NZP; **169** Chris Schmitz, NTWP (t,b); **170–171** AA, © 1995 Breck P. Kent (l), PhotoDisc, Inc.‡ (c), AA, © 1995 Alan G. Nelson (r); **172** Jessie Cohen, NZP (t,bl,br); **173** Jessie Cohen, NZP (tl,tr,b); **175** Gary Kramer, NTWP; **176** PhotoDisc, Inc.‡; **177** Jessie Cohen, NZP; **178** Jessie Cohen, NZP (l,r); **179** AA, © 1995 Michael Dick (t), AA, © 1995 Michael Dick (b); **180** © ZSSD (tl), Ron Garrison, © ZSSD (tr), © ZSSD (b); **181** © Peter Kresan (tl), Ron Magill, MMZ (tr), © ZSSD (m,b); **182** David Erikson, USFWS (t), PhotoDisc, Inc.‡ (b); **183** PhotoDisc, Inc.‡; **184** USFWS; **185** USFWS (t), PhotoDisc, Inc.‡ (b); **186** USFWS (l), Ron Garrison, © ZSSD (r); **187** NTWP; **188** AA, © 1995 Robert Maier (t), Chris Schmitz, NTWP (b); **189** USFWS (l), PhotoDisc, Inc.‡ (r); **190** PhotoDisc, Inc.‡ (tl,tr), Craig Koppie, USFWS (b); **191** Ron Garrison, © ZSSD (l,r); **193** Bob Couey, SWC**; **194** USFWS (t,b); **195** Bob Couey, SWC**; **196** USFWS (t), PhotoDisc, Inc.‡ (b); **197** AA, © 1995 Norbert Rosing, Oxford Scientific Films; **198** USFWS (t,b); **199** AA, © 1995 Brian Milne; **200** Brian O'Donnell, USFWS; **201** Sea World Florida† (t); **202** Bob Couey, SWC**; **203** USFWS (t), Sea World Florida† (m), Bob Couey, SWC** (b); **204** Bob Couey, SWC** (tl,b), PhotoDisc, Inc.‡ (tr); **205** Larry R. Nygren, USFWS; **206** Bob Couey, SWC** (l,r); **207** Bob Couey, SWC** (t,b); **208** Jim Leupold, USFWS (tl), Bob Couey, SWC** (tr), Lance Kenyon, NTWP (b)**Glossary: amphibian** Jessie Cohen, NZP; **arid** PhotoDisc, Inc.‡; **big cat** Jessie Cohen, NZP; **bird of prey** Jessie Cohen, NZP; **buttress** Jessie Cohen, NZP; **cold-blooded** Jessie Cohen, NZP; **endangered species** Jessie Cohen, NZP; **epiphyte** PhotoDisc, Inc.‡; **extinct** *Animals: 1419 Copyright -Free Illustrations of Mammals, Birds, Fish, Insects, etc.* by Jim Harter, published by Dover Publications, Inc.; **herbivorous** FRWC; **immersion exhibit** Jessie Cohen, NZP; **invertebrate** Jessie Cohen, NZP; **mammal** Jessie Cohen, NZP; **molt** Jessie Cohen, NZP; **mustelid** NPS photo; **night vision** PhotoDisc, Inc.‡; **primate** PhotoDisc, Inc.‡; **regurgitate** Bob Couey, SWC**; **rodent** NPS; **small cat** Ron Garrison, © ZSSD; **ungulate** Jessie Cohen, NZP; **zygodactyl** © ZSSD.

More About Zoo Animals

Attenborough, David. *The Living Planet*. Boston: Little, Brown, 1984.

Benyus, Janine M. *Beastly Behaviors*. Reading, Mass.: Addison-Wesley, 1992.

Hare, Tony, ed. *Habitats*. New York: Macmillan Inc., 1994.

Koebner, Linda. *Zoo: The Evolution of Wildlife Conservation Centers*. New York: Tom Doherty Associates Inc., 1994.

MacDonald, David, ed. *Encyclopedia of Mammals*. New York: Van Nostrand Reinhold, 1979.

Page, Jake. *Smithsonian's New Zoo*. Washington, D.C.: Smithsonian Institution Press, 1990.

Parker, Sybil P., ed. *Grzimek's Encyclopedia of Mammals*. (English language edition) New York: McGraw-Hill, 1990.

Contributors

Design	Production	Editorial
Lisa Rosowsky	Paul Farwell	Jacqueline Bigford
	Marguerite Meister	Sue Causey-Foley
	Aleksander Nowicki	Benjamin Chadwick
		Robert Costello
		Kristen Holmstrand
		Elizabeth Mitchell
		Michael Pistrich
		Jane Redmont
		Hilary Sardella
		Barbara Simons

a pool

Sun bittern

Fiberglass kapok tree

Titi monkey

The trunk of the kapok "tree" (above) is fiberglass, cast from molds made of a living tree in the tropics. The trunk houses part of the heating and air-conditioning systems, and provides structural support. It also forms the base for plants and vines, and is a home for monkeys.

Mountain g

In the last few decades a new philosophy of presenting animals within their natural habitat has gained ground. In modern zoological parks, animals are provided with homes that closely match their surroundings in the wild. This change in philosophy is partially the result of a better understanding of habitats and of the part zoos can play in conserving wildlife.

Zoo exhibits now bring together animals, plants, and insects from a single habitat into a rich mix approximating their life in the wild. To accomplish this requires a great deal of creativity, planning, and building. Every aspect of the habitat must be reproduced, including temperature and humidity,

Cliffs sculpted from concrete create an environment for mountain goats at Woodland Park Zoo in Seattle.

Greater kudus—Busch Gardens

Greater kudus (above) mix with several species of antelope in the African Plains exhibit at Busch Gardens in Florida. A hollow tree (right) serves as a home for an elf owl at the Arizona–Sonora Desert Museum.

at—Woodland Park Zoo

Elf owl—Arizona

rainfall and soil conditions. The difficulty of reproducing a desert or tropical environment in a northern city with cold winters cannot be underestimated.

Amazonia, a tropical forest exhibit at the Smithsonian Institution's National Zoo, contains 358 plant species and about 100 species of mammals and birds. The Brookfield Zoo's Habitat Africa! exhibit includes a 170 foot (52 m) long water-hole and a rocky outcrop where various animal species gather and interact on the African savannah. At the Metro Toronto Zoo's Indo-Malaya Pavilion, birds from India and Sri Lanka fly freely among banyan trees in a 65 foot (20 m) tall exhibit.